Fresh Packet of Sower's Seeds
Third Planting

by

Brian Cavanaugh, T.O.R.

Paulist Press
New York　Mahwah

Library of Congress Cataloging-in-Publication Data

Fresh packet of sower's seeds : third planting / [edited] by Brian Cavanaugh.
    p.   cm.
    Includes index.
    ISBN 0-8091-3491-8 :
    1. Homiletical illustrations. I. Cavanaugh, Brian, 1947– .
BV4225.2.F74   1994
251'.08—dc20
                                94-14485
                                    CIP

Published by Paulist Press
997 Macarthur Boulevard
Mahwah, NJ 07430

Printed and bound in the
United States of America

Contents

Dedication

This book is dedicated to Joe Loizzo and Fr. Dan Sinisi, TOR. These two men have been instrumental in helping me arrive at some understanding of this part of my life journey. They both were there for me at critical moments to listen and encourage. I thank them. I hope these stories can be of some help to other men and women who are going through transition times in life.

Acknowledgments

I am very grateful for all those people who purchased my first two books—*The Sower's Seeds* and *More Sower's Seeds: Second Planting*. They are, as well, now being printed in India and the Philippines by the Society of St. Paul in arrangements with Paulist Press.

Once again I am indebted to Donna Menis for her expertise in editing the manuscript and providing insights and suggestions that enhanced the final copy. Also, I am grateful for Maria Maggi, my editor at Paulist Press, for her patience and persistence in bringing this book to publication.

Thank you, Joe, Dan, Donna and Maria. Without your assistance *Fresh Packet of Sower's Seeds: Third Planting* would not have been ready for the next planting season.

Introduction

"Lazarus, Come Out!"
Unraveling or Unbinding?

Have you ever had someone tell you, "You must be going through one of those life-building opportunities, or a growth experience"? Transition times in life are certainly among those opportunities and they can jolt a person into a new understanding of life's experiences. I was in the final stages of compiling this book when I had the opportunity to experience one of life's transitions. I was moving from an educational assignment where I had been stationed for ten and one-half years to another educational institution. By way of a story, I will try to relate my journey toward integrating this experience in my life.

I was driving home after an interview for the new position; my thoughts were spinning around in my head like a band of whirling dervishes. The thought of leaving where I had been for over ten years was not appealing. I began to question my hesitation about leaving. Was it because I was too comfortable and secure where I was? Was I afraid to take a risk?

My own self-talk started to kick in, the kinds of things I would tell to students who come to me when they are faced with major decisions: "Nothing significant in life occurs in the comfort zone. We have to get out of the ruts and get into the risk zone. Only in the risk zone will we find success and accomplishments in life." I realized that if my hesitations toward this new assignment arose simply because I was too comfortable and too secure where I was, then I would

1

no longer be able to give another one of my motivational/ inspirational talks.

This whole experience began during Holy Week, and the image of Lazarus in the tomb took on a new significance for me. No longer was it just a biblical story. It was becoming a personal episode filled with new insights. I felt Jesus was calling me to come out of my tomb. I heard my response, "Say what, Jesus? You want me to come out where? It's too bright out there. Besides, it's nice and secure in here. I'm quite comfortable, thank you."

"Come out!" Jesus seemed to say again. And the next words Jesus says are critical, "Unbind him, and let him go" (Jn 11:43, 44 RSV). You see, Lazarus could not unbind himself and set himself free. Likewise, we cannot unbind and free ourselves from whatever it is that binds us. So I began to ask myself: "What are my bindings? Is there any difference in the shells I built to isolate and insulate myself from others than in the bindings of Lazarus? Just what is binding me in the tomb of comfort and security?"

Slowly, as if in the midst of a morning fog lifting, it dawned on me that the shells I use to insulate and isolate myself from so many things were no different than Lazarus' tomb and bindings. They were constructed to shield and protect but, actually, they shut me off and denied my freedom rather than setting me free.

So, I accepted the new assignment. After all was said and done, I felt I understood this Lazarus story well enough. Right? I learned I had to shed these shells that were binding me. I had to get out of the security of my comfort zone and step out into the risk zone of new ventures, *or so I thought.* Shortly after arriving at my new assignment, however, this transition took a strange twist. The nice, neat, tidy ending became unglued.

I shared my interpretation of the Lazarus story with several of the people at my new assignment with whom I felt comfortable. I let them know that this was a big risk for me to let go of these bindings, and that I would probably need help with the unbinding process. The exact sequence of events that occurred over the next few days is a blur. It seemed that my life started to spin out of control. Past fears, failures, and dragons from that dark place we like to keep shut off arose and began to twist and turn me. I could describe my feelings only in terms of spinning out of control, tumbling down a deep dark hole, and not being able to grasp onto anything to hold.

Fortunately, someone mentioned the name of a staff counselor and he made the time to speak with me. Between the many visits with the counselor, and assistance from a discerning spiritual director, I was helped to understand this experience more as unraveling rather than unbinding. Too many changes were happening too fast and they had activated my internal "tilt" signal.

I came to understand that there is a distinct difference between unraveling out of control and being set free by a slow unbinding. First, the process of setting free cannot be done by oneself. We need the assistance of another person to help us listen to ourselves and ask some of those "tough questions." Second, unbinding is often painful, especially with those bindings closest to our "self." It is a slow process to loosen the grip of the bindings which took years to harden into a shell. Third, unraveling is like spinning a top—one end is grabbed and then it is yanked hard. However, it usually spins out of control, going this way and that, with no clear direction. Such is the case when one's life seems to be unraveling and spinning out of control.

Finally, there is no nice, neat, tidy, "lived happily ever after," ending to this story. The unbinding process continues. I persevere on this journey toward understanding and integration. One thing I can tell you is that there is a distinct difference between unraveling and unbinding. Yes, I still hear that voice calling, "Come out!" And it is risky to shed the additional layers of my shells, and to allow more bindings to be unbound. However, the journey is much easier knowing there are people who care enough to undergo the messy process of unbinding in order to help set me free and people who will act as guides on this journey toward understanding and integration. So I can begin a new day in the face of the Risen Sun.

If my interpretation of the Lazarus story resonates within your heart where comfort and security have become more of a tomb, hear Jesus' words calling out to you: "Come out!"

1.
Do What Needs To Be Done

Anonymous

A young man answered a want-ad for a farmhand. He told the owner about his previous work experience and then added, "And I can sleep when the wind blows." This puzzled the farmer a bit. However, he needed the help, so he hired the young man.

During the next few months the hired hand did everything asked of him, and the farmer was satisfied.

Late one night, one of those infamous midwestern windstorms roared across the plains. It was two in the morning, but the farmer got up, put on his clothes and ran out to tie down whatever needed to be secured. First, he checked the barn. The doors were shut tight, shutters were closed, and the animals were all properly tied in their stalls. He checked the springhouse, the pump, the storage shed, the machinery, and the trucks. All was secured.

The farmer frantically ran from place to place. He just knew something had to be loose, uncovered, or rattling. However, everything was as it should be. The farmer then stuck his head into the bunkhouse to thank the new hand, only to find him sound asleep.

Then the farmer remembered that curious statement, "I can sleep when the wind blows." He smiled, realizing that the young man had done everything he was expected to do. He could, indeed, sleep when the wind blew.

2.
Consider the Walnut

Anonymous

Consider the walnut! If you compare a walnut with some of the beautiful and exciting things that grow on our planet, it does not seem to be a marvelous act of creation. It is common looking, rough, not particularly attractive, and certainly not monetarily valuable.

Besides, it is small. Its growth is limited by the hard shell that surrounds it, the shell from which it never escapes on its own.

Of course, though, that's the wrong way to judge a walnut.

Break a walnut open and look inside. See how the walnut has grown to fill every nook and cranny available to it. It had no say in the size or shape of that shell, but, given those limitations, it achieved its full potential of growth.

How lucky we will be if, like the walnut, we blossom and bloom in every space of life that is given to us.

Take heart! If one nut can do it, so can you.

3.
The Gospel According to You

Anonymous

The gospels of Matthew, Mark, Luke and John
Are read by more than a few,
But the one that is most read and commented on
Is the gospel according to you.
You are writing a gospel, a chapter each day
By the things that you do and the words that you say.
People read what you write, whether faithless or true.
Say, what is the gospel according to you?

Do others read His truth and His love in your life?
Or has yours been too full of malice and strife?
Does your life speak of evil, or does it ring true?
Say, what is the gospel according to you?

4.
Giving or Keeping

Anonymous

I read somewhere that the Sea of Galilee and the Dead Sea are formed by the same water supply. It flows down, clear and cool, from Mount Hermon. The Sea of Galilee makes beauty of its water, for the sea has an outlet. It gets to give. It gathers in its riches that it may pour them out again to fertilize the Jordan plain.

The Dead Sea, on the other hand, with the same source of refreshing water, is desolate, for the Dead Sea has no outlet. It gets only to keep.

Interestingly, unselfish and selfish people act much the same way. Unselfish people get to give and luxuriate in their generosity while selfish people only get to keep and stagnate into desolation.

5.
Chuck Yeager—The Right Stuff

Chuck Yeager

Chuck Yeager relates in his autobiography, *Yeager*, "The question I'm asked most often is whether I think I've got 'the right stuff.' "

Yeager continues, "The question annoys me because it implies that someone who has 'the right stuff' was born that way. I was born with unusually good eyes and coordination.

7

I was mechanically gifted and understood machines easily. My nature was to stay cool in tight spots. Is that 'the right stuff'?

"All I know is, I worked my tail off to learn how to fly, and worked hard at it all the way. And in the end, the one big reason why I was better than average as a pilot was because I flew more often than anyone else. If there is such a thing as 'the right stuff' in piloting, then it is experience."

6.
Alphabet Prayer

Anonymous

One night while babysitting, a grandfather passed his granddaughter's room and overheard her repeating the alphabet in an oddly reverent fashion. "What on earth are you up to?" he asked.

"I'm saying my prayers," explained the little girl. "But I can't think of exactly the right words tonight, so I'm just saying all the letters. God will put them together for me, because he knows what I'm thinking."

7.
Conquer Weaknesses

Anonymous

Lord Nelson, England's famous naval hero, suffered from seasickness throughout his entire life. Needless to say, the man who destroyed Napoleon's fleet did not let it interfere with his career and duties. He not only learned to live with this personal weakness, he conquered it.

8.
We've Lost Sight of Christmas

Brian Cavanaugh, T.O.R.

During the frenzied pace of the Christmas season, we tend to lose sight of the message and promise that Christmas heralds. So often we're caught up in getting ready for this's and last minute that's. We rush here. We push there, and practically run over people seeking that special gift which we really cannot afford.

Could all this hurrying and scurrying be Satan's vengeance against God, or his revenge against the Incarnation—the birth of the Son of God? Satan blinds us all with the glitter and gloss, sounds of bells tingling and cash registers jingling. We've lost sight of the meaning of Christmas—the message of peace among all men and women, the promise of joy to everyone of good will.

Christmas' true splendor is found more often in simplicity—simplicity rooted in awareness and listening. For as we listen more to the world around us, we become increasingly aware of the troubles and pain, the anger and strain that men and women suffer. It is the message and promise of Christmas which can bring hope to the little, the lost and the least; to the bruised, the battered and the broken.

One of the greatest gifts we can bring to the world, bring to each man, woman or child we meet this Christmas season, is to "practice random kindness and senseless acts of beauty." I'm reminded of the *B.C.* comic strip from several years ago in which cartoonist Johnny Hart has the character Wiley searching for answers to one of life's great questions. It is a question so simple and yet so timely. In the first panel Wiley asks, "Whatever happened to kindness?" He then proceeds to write the following verse:

> "Why do people go to the trouble
> to give other people some trouble?

Why do they burst someone's bubble,
    when they know it comes back to them double?
Why do we go to the effort to hurt
    someone we actually love?
Why can't we say something sweet 'stead of curt?
    A push only leads to a shove.
Why can't we treat other folks with respect?
    With a smile or a kind word or two?
Treat them with honor, the way you'd expect
    they should act when they're dealing with you.
Why can't we overlook others' mistakes?
    We've all surely been there before.
Love and forgiveness is all that it takes,
    to boot Satan's butt out the door."

This Christmas season, give a gift that will last, a gift that will endure long after you are gone. "Practice random kindness and senseless acts of beauty." Go ahead, try it! It will shock you only a bit. I'm sure it will astound others, too, and I am certain it will startle the world around you. Go ahead, practice kindness anyway. The world could use a jolt such as this.

9.
Art Is So Easy

Anonymous

A young woman was visiting Michelangelo in his sculpting studio. She was fascinated watching him work, and said, "I never knew sculpting was so easy. Why, I bet I could do that, too."

"Sure, nothing to it," replied Michelangelo. "All you need is a block of marble, a hammer and a chisel. Then you simply knock off all the marble which you don't want."

10.
The Priceless Ingredient

Anonymous

There is an old Sufi tale set in Baghdad. In the city lived Hakeem, The Wise One, to whom many people came for counsel and advice. He gave it freely, asking nothing in return.

One day a young man came to him. The young man had squandered much of his life and had little to show for it. He inquired of Hakeem, "Tell me, Wise One, what shall I do to receive the most for what I do with my life?"

Hakeem answered, "A thing that is bought or sold has no value unless it contains that which cannot be bought or sold. Look for the priceless ingredient."

"But what is this 'priceless' ingredient?" asked the young man.

The Wise One said, "My son, the priceless ingredient is the honor and integrity of those who make the product. Consider this well before you buy."

Yes, each of us might well consider this for our own lives. Honor and integrity are the priceless ingredients which will return the most to us.

11.
A Mother's Paraphrase of 1 Corinthians 13

Mrs. Mervin Seashore

Though I speak with the language of educators and psychiatrists and have not love, I am as blaring brass or a crashing cymbal.

And if I have the gift of planning my child's future and understanding all the mysteries of the child's mind and have ample knowledge of teenagers, and though I have all faith in my

11

children, so that I could remove their mountains of doubts and fears and have not love, I am nothing.

And though I bestow all my goods to feed and nourish them properly, and though I give my body to backbreaking housework and have not love, it profits me not.

Love is patient with the naughty child and is kind. Love does not envy when a child wants to move to grandma's house because "she is nice."

Love is not anxious to impress a teenager with one's superior knowledge.

Love has good manners in the home—does not act selfishly or with a martyr complex, is not easily provoked by normal childish actions.

Love does not remember the wrongs of yesterday and love thinks no evil—it gives the child the benefit of the doubt.

Love does not make light of sin in the child's life (or in her own, either), but rejoices when he or she comes to a knowledge of the truth.

Love does not fail. Whether there be comfortable surroundings, they shall fail; whether there be total communication between parents and children, it will cease; whether there be good education, it shall vanish.

When we were children, we spoke and acted and understood as children, but now that we have become parents, we must act maturely.

Now abides faith, hope, and love—these three are needed in the home. Faith in Jesus Christ, eternal hope for the future of the child, and God's love shed in our hearts, but the greatest of these is love.

12.
With Enthusiasm

Anonymous

A jeweler to the rich and famous once sold a magnificent ruby to a customer after one of her sales clerks had failed to interest the same customer. Asked how she did it, the jeweler said, "My sales clerk is excellent, an expert on precious stones. There's just one difference between us. He knows jewels, but I love them. I care what happens to them, who wears them. The customers sense this. It makes them want to buy—and they do."

13.
The Tiger Cub That Roared

Anonymous

There's a fable about a scrawny tiger cub that was abandoned by its mother shortly after birth, and was raised by a friendly herd of goats. All day, every day, the cub played with the goat kids, drank the nanny's milk, and slept in the goats' cave.

In time, the cub came to think of itself as one of the goats. It would try as hard as it could to bleat like a goat, to cultivate a taste for grass and twigs, and to leap in the air like any normal goat. But, somehow, the tiger cub could never quite get the hang of it all.

One day, a huge Bengal tiger bounded out from the trees into the clearing where the cub and the goats were playing. It let out a tremendous roar. All the goats fled in terror for cover, but, for some strange reason, the little tiger felt drawn to the magnificent animal.

The big tiger led the little tiger down to a nearby stream and suggested that the cub take a look at its reflection in the water. The cub was amazed at the sight. Then the big tiger sat back on its haunches and let out a jungle-shaking roar. "There," it taunted, "why don't you try to roar like that?"

The little tiger cub mimicked the big tiger, sitting back and straining as hard as it could. Eventually, it felt a whisper deep within its throat. It grew stronger and stronger, until at last, the cub opened its mouth wide and let out a jungle-shaking roar of its own.

From that day forward, so the fable goes, the tiger cub knew it could never again live like a goat.

14.
The Brilliant Illiterate

Anonymous

The minister of a local church insisted on leaving written instructions and notes to his staff. A janitor who could not read or write was soon found out when he failed to respond to the written messages. He lost his job.

Although unlettered, he was brilliant and soon began his own business and became very wealthy. One day his banker was astonished to discover his illiteracy. The banker said, "Good heavens, just imagine where you would be if you could read and write."

The successful man grinned and said, "Yup, I'd be a janitor in an Episcopal church."

15.
Town with Four Neighborhoods (adapted)

Jim Savage

There is a town that has four separate neighborhoods. The first neighborhood is called, "Yabuts." The people who live there think they know what needs to be done. As a matter of fact, they talk about it quite convincingly—up to a point. When told they have an opportunity for something, the conversation goes something like this: "Ya, but . . ." The "Ya-buts" have the answer. It just happens to be the wrong answer.

The next neighborhood is known as the "Gunnados." Now they are some of the best-intentioned folks you could ever meet. They really understand what needs to be done, and they would have done it, if they had only followed through. They study everything that is required very carefully, and just as an opportunity drifts past them, they realize what they were "gunnado." If only they had done what they were "gunnado."

Another neighborhood is known as the "Wishawoodas." These people have an excellent perspective on life—hindsight. They say, "I 'wishawooda' this, or 'wishawooda' that. . . ." They know everything that should be done, only it's after the fact.

The last neighborhood is known as the "Gladidids." They are a truly special group of people. The "Wishawoodas" drive by the "Gladidids' " homes and admire them. The "Gunnados" want to join them, but just cannot quite get around to it. The "Yabuts" could have been "Gladidids," but destiny just did not smile on them. The "Gladidids" are pleased that they are disciplined enough to do what they know they should do instead of always doing what they wanted to do.

These are the four neighborhoods. In which neighborhood do you live? In which one would you rather live?

16.
Art of Conversation

Anonymous

A college professor was approached by a student who queried, "Conversational ability is crucial for success in my future profession, yet there are no such courses offered. How can I learn the art of conversation?"

"A good question," replied the professor, "and if you will just listen, I will tell you how."

There ensued a long and awkward silence. Finally the student interrupted, saying, "Well, I'm listening."

"You see," said the professor, "already you are learning."

17.
Planting Big Potatoes

Anonymous

Many years ago Irish immigrants subscribed to the theory that they could eat all the big potatoes and keep the small potatoes for seed planting. They did this for quite some time. They ate the big potatoes; they planted the small potatoes. Soon, however, greater understanding of the laws of nature came to them, for while they kept up this practice, nature reduced all their potatoes to the size of marbles. The Irish farmers learned through bitter experience that they could not keep the best things of life for themselves and use the leftovers for seed. The laws of nature decreed that the harvest would reflect the planting season.

Planting small potatoes is still common practice today. We often try to keep the best things of life for ourselves and to plant inferior things. We expect that by some crazy twist of the laws of nature our own selfishness will reward us with unselfishness. Is this not true in terms of time, personal talents, serving others, sharing our faith, living according to the Golden Rule?

We need to remember what the Irish farmers learned: we cannot eat all the big potatoes and still keep on having them through the years. Truly the harvest reflects the planting season.

Ask yourself, What am I planting in life? What does my

harvest reflect—what I have already, or the harvest that is yet to be? For it can only be "as you sow, so you will reap."

18.
Attitude Determines Response

Anonymous

A young boy sat on the front porch of a farmhouse with his grandfather. They heard a car coming down the seldom traveled dirt road that passed close to the farmhouse. When the driver of the car, bearing out-of-state plates, saw them on the front porch, he stopped to ask directions to a nearby town.

After receiving directions from the old-timer, the driver walked back toward his car. He had walked only a few steps when he hesitated, and awkwardly inquired of the old man, "Say, mister, what are the folks like around here?"

"Why do you ask?" the grandfather responded.

Taking a few steps closer, the stranger said, "I just left a town where the people were a bunch of snobs. I've never been around people who were less friendly in my life." The stranger went on, "Why, I lived in that town for over a year, and never once did I feel a part of the community."

"I guess that's about the way you'll find folks around here to be also," the old man replied.

The stranger said his goodbyes and drove away. The grandson looked puzzled, but said nothing.

A few hours later, another car stopped in front of the farmhouse where the two of them still sat on the porch. The driver, with a big smile on her face, strolled briskly up the front walk and asked directions to the same town. After carefully writing down the directions, she, too, inquired, "Tell me, what are the folks around here like?"

Once again the old farmer questioned, "Why do you ask?"

"You see, I'm moving here from one of the nicest little

towns you could ask for," the woman answered with a smile. "The people made me feel so much at home there. The neighbors were so friendly. I felt I had lived there all my life."

"Well," said the old man, "you'll find the people around here pretty much the same."

The woman got into her car and drove off. The boy turned to his grandfather with a puzzled expression and asked, "Grandpa, why did you give those two strangers opposite answers to the same question?"

The grandfather put his hand on the boy's shoulder and answered, "Because, laddie, it's a person's attitude toward a community that determines how the people will respond to them. People all across the country are pretty much the same."

19.
A Leader Knows

Chinese Proverb

An old Chinese proverb on leadership states:

He who knows and knows not that he knows; he is
    asleep, wake him.
He who knows not and knows not that he knows not;
    he is a fool, shun him.
He who knows not and knows that he knows not; he is
    a child, teach him.
He who knows and knows that he knows; he is a
    leader, follow him.

20.
Unnoticed Value

Anonymous

Some time ago, one of the wire services carried this story: "For several years a 14-inch statue was used as a doorstop in the home of Leo Casey of Green Township, Ohio. It was not until Casey's estate was appraised after his death that someone recognized the item as a miniature replica of Rodin's classic sculpture, *The Thinker*, a masterpiece created in the 19th century. When art dealers appraised the miniature statue, they valued its worth at $16,000."

21.
Where Are Your Abilities?

Anonymous

In 1904, a Texas farmer was going broke. His farm suffered from a catastrophic drought. The crops were shriveling in the fields and the cattle became diseased. In desperation he made a deal with a large oil corporation, which believed there might be oil on his land. The deal stated that the farmer would set up and operate the drilling rig, financed by the oil company. If the farmer struck oil, he would receive a hefty percentage from the oil profits.

The Texas farmer really had no choice. He was deeply in debt trying to scratch out a living from the craggy land. Much to his surprise and elation, he struck oil within a few months.

Actually large quantities of oil had been under the farm all the time, while he and his family were starving to death trying to farm the land.

Individual abilities and talents are very much like that oil well. Usually they are just beneath the surface waiting to be discovered, mostly in times of adversity.

22.
Letter on Humility (XIV)

C. S. Lewis

My dear Wormwood, The most alarming thing in your last account of the patient is that he is making none of those confident resolutions which marked his original conversion. No more lavish promises of perpetual virtue, I gather; not even the expectation of an endowment of "grace" for life, but only a hope for the daily and hourly pittance to meet the daily and hourly temptation! This is very bad.

I see only one thing to do at the moment. Your patient has become humble; have you drawn his attention to the fact? All virtues are formidable to us once the [human] is aware that he has them, but this is specially true of humility. Catch him at the moment when he is really poor in spirit and smuggle into his mind the gratifying reflection, "By jove! I'm being humble," and almost immediately pride—pride at his own humility—will appear. If he awakes to the danger and tries to smother this new form of pride, make him proud of his attempt—and so on, through as many stages as you please. . . .

You must . . . conceal from the patient the true end of humility. Let him think of it, not as self-forgetfulness, but as a certain kind of opinion (namely, a low opinion) of his own talents and character. Some talents, I gather, he really has. Fix in his mind the idea that humility consists in trying to believe those talents to be less valuable than he believes them to be. No doubt they *are* in fact less valuable than he believes, but that is not the point. The great thing is to make him value an opinion for some quality other than truth, thus introducing an element of dishonesty and make-believe into the heart of what otherwise threatens to become a virtue. By this method thousands of humans have been brought to think that humility means pretty women trying to believe they are ugly and clever men trying to believe they are fools. And since what they are trying to believe may, in some cases, be manifest nonsense, they cannot succeed in believing it, and we have the chance of keeping their minds endlessly revolving on themselves in an effort to achieve the impossible. To anticipate the Enemy's strategy [God's, remember?], we must consider His aims. . . . The Enemy wants him, in the end, to be so free from any bias in his own favor that he can rejoice in his own talents as frankly and gratefully as in his neighbor's talents—

or in a sunrise, an elephant, or a waterfall. He wants each [human] in the long run to be able to recognize all creatures (even himself) as glorious and excellent things . . . but it is His long-term policy, I fear, to restore to them a new kind of self-love—a charity and gratitude for all selves, including their own; when they have really learned to love their neighbors as themselves. For we must never forget what is the most repellant and inexplicable trait in our Enemy; He *really* loves the hairless bipeds he has created. . . .

His whole effort, therefore, will be to get the man's mind off the subject of his own value altogether. He would rather the man thought himself a great architect or a great poet and then forget about it, than that he should spend much time and pains trying to think himself a bad one. Your efforts to instil either vainglory or false modesty into the patient will therefore be met from the Enemy's side with the obvious reminder that a [human] is not usually called upon to have an opinion of his own talents at all, since he can very well go on improving them to the best of his ability without deciding on his own niche in the temple of fame. You must try to exclude this reminder from the patient's consciousness at all costs. . . . But always and by all methods the Enemy's aim will be to get the patient's mind off such questions, and yours will be to fix it on them. Even of his sins the Enemy does not want him to think too much: once they are repented, the sooner the man turns his attention outward, the better the Enemy is pleased.

Your affectionate uncle,
Screwtape

23.
Companions—"With Bread" (adapted)

Rev. Robert McAfee Brown

The Rev. Robert McAfee Brown in an essay in *Life* magazine addressed the question, "What is the meaning of life?"

21

He wrote: "I believe we are placed here to be companions—a wonderful word that comes from the Latin *cum panis,* 'with bread.' We are here to share bread with one another so that everyone has enough, no one has too much. Our social order achieves this goal with maximum freedom and minimum coercion.

"There are many names for such sharing companions: the Body of Christ, the Kingdom of God, the Communion of Saints. And while the goal is too vast to be realized fully on this planet, it is still our task to create foretastes of it in this world. We are to generate living glimpses of what life is meant to be, which include art, music, poetry and shared laughter and moral outrages and special privileges for children only, and wonder, humor and endless love—to counterbalance the otherwise immobilizing realities of tyrants, starving children, senseless death and just plain greed.

"We are here to be companions along the journey of life, to share bread with one another, to 'build up the Kingdom of God here on earth as it is in heaven,' to love one another as Jesus first loved you."

24.
Fulfilled Dreams, Burning Desire

Anonymous

To a certain young boy, the Cleveland Browns were more than just a football team. The Browns had on their roster the great running back, Jimmy Brown. When the Browns played in Los Angeles, the boy, who considered Jimmy Brown a hero, stood at the locker room door waiting for the Cleveland team to finish dressing after a game.

Suddenly his hero appeared in the doorway, bigger than life. The youngster was awestruck. Nervously he blurted out, "Mr. Brown, Mr. Brown, you're my hero!"

"Yeah, sure kid," Brown mumbled while signing autographs.

Intent on getting his attention, the boy said, "Mr. Brown, I've collected all your football cards, know all your records by heart, and watch you whenever I can."

Brown, somewhat disturbed by the boy's persistence, grunted back, "Great, kid. Keep me in your dreams."

Finally, the determined kid tugged on Jimmy Brown's coat and said, "Mr. Brown, I not only know your records, but I plan to break every one of them."

Jimmy Brown stopped in his tracks, knelt down, and looked this kid squarely in the eyes. "What's your name, kid?" Brown respectfully asked.

The youngster knew he had Jimmy Brown's attention now. "My name is Simpson, sir. My friends just call me O.J."

25.
Vision of the Snail

Anonymous

One raw, windy day in spring, a snail started to climb a cherry tree. Some birds in a nearby tree sniped their ridicule. "Hey, you dumb snail," squawked one of them, "where do you think you're going?" "Why are you climbing that tree?" others chimed in. "There are no cherries on it."

"There will be some by the time I get there," replied the snail.

26.
Teller of New Truths

Merle Crowell

There is a story about a Greenland Eskimo who was taken on one of the American polar expeditions. As a reward for his faithful service, he was brought to New York City for a short visit. He was filled with wonder at all the miracles of sight and sound. When he returned to his native village, he told stories of buildings that rose into the very face of the sky. He spoke of streetcars, which he described as houses that moved along the trail, with people living in them as they moved. He told about mammoth bridges, artificial lights, and all the other dazzling delights of the great metropolis.

His people looked at him coldly and walked away. Throughout the village he was dubbed, "The Liar." This name he carried in shame to this grave. Long before his death, his original name was entirely forgotten in the village.

When Knud Rasmussen made his trip from Greenland to Alaska, he was accompanied by an Eskimo named Mitek from the same village. Mitek visited Copenhagen and New York, where he saw many things for the first time and was duly impressed. Later, upon his return to Greenland, he recalled the tragedy of "The Liar" and decided that it would not be wise to tell the truth. Instead, he narrated stories that his people could grasp and thus saved his reputation.

He told them how he and Dr. Rasmussen maintained a kayak on the banks of a great river, the Hudson, and how each morning they paddled out for their hunting; ducks, geese and seals were plentiful. And Mitek said they enjoyed the visit with the "natives" immensely.

Mitek, in the eyes of his village, was a very honest man. His neighbors treated him with rare respect.

27.
Tragedy or Blessing?

Anonymous

Years ago in Scotland, the Clark family had a dream. Clark and his wife worked and saved, making plans for their family of nine children to travel to the United States. It had taken years, but they had finally saved enough money. They got their passports and made reservations for the family on a new ocean liner.

The entire family was filled with anticipation and excitement about their venture. However, several days before the departure, the youngest son was bitten by a dog. The doctor stitched the leg, but hung a yellow flag on the Clark's front door. Because of the possibility of rabies, the entire family was quarantined for 14 days.

The family's dream was dashed. They would not be able to make the trip to America as planned. The father, filled with disappointment and anger, stomped to the dock to watch the ship leave—without the Clark family. The father shed bitter tears and cursed his son and God for their misfortune.

Five days later, the tragic news spread throughout Scotland and the world—the mighty *Titanic* had sunk. The unsinkable ship had sunk, taking hundreds of lives with it. The Clark family was to have been on that ship, but because their son had been bitten by a dog, they were left behind.

When Mr. Clark heard the news, he hugged his son, and gave thanks to God for saving his family and turning what was believed to have been a tragedy into a blessing.

28.
Art of Leadership

Anonymous

When addressing his young officers, General Dwight D. Eisenhower used to demonstrate the art of leadership with a simple piece of string. He would place a length of string in front of each officer and say, "Pull the string and it will follow wherever you wish to lead it. Now push the string, and it goes nowhere at all."

Eisenhower slowly looked each officer in the eye and said, "It's just the same when it comes to leading people."

29.
The Miracle Bridge

Anonymous

The Brooklyn Bridge that spans the river between Manhattan and Brooklyn is simply an engineering miracle. In 1883, a creative engineer, John Roebling, was inspired by an idea for this spectacular bridge project. However, bridge-building experts told him to forget it, it just was not possible.

Roebling convinced his son, Washington, an up-and-coming engineer, that the bridge could be built. The two of them conceived the concept of how it could be accomplished, and how to overcome the obstacles. Somehow they convinced bankers to finance the project. Now with unharnessed excitement and energy, they hired their crew and began to build their dream bridge.

The project was only a few months underway when a tragic on-site accident killed John Roebling and severely injured his son. Washington was severely brain-damaged, unable to talk or walk. Everyone thought that the project would have to be scrapped since the Roeblings were the only ones who understood how the bridge could be built.

Though Washington Roebling was unable to move or talk, his mind was as sharp as ever. He still had a fierce determination to complete the bridge. One day, as he lay in his hospital bed, an idea flashed in his mind as to how to develop a communication code. All he could move was one finger, so he touched the arm of his wife with that finger. He tapped out the code to communicate to her what she was to tell the engineers who continued building the bridge. For thirteen years, Washington tapped out his instructions with one finger until the spectacular Brooklyn Bridge was finally completed.

30.
"Metamorphosis"

Anonymous

"Metamorphosis" is a story about an unmarried man, Gregor, who lives with his parents and sister. For years he's been a salesman, a slave to his boss and to his customers. He smiles on the outside, but inside he's unhappy. He feels like an insect. Each night he dreams of his insect-like life. Then one morning he wakes up to discover that he's become what he feels like: a giant cockroach.

The tragedy is that the only way Gregor can become human again is if he is loved by humans, especially his family. But his appearance makes this impossible. The greater part of the story deals with Gregor's pathetic efforts to express himself to his family. Ultimately, he simply gives up and dies, remaining a cockroach until the end.

31.
The Errant Knight of Assisi

Brian Cavanaugh, T.O.R.

There is a chapter in the Book of the Ages that tells the tale of a weary knight who rode his tired horse down an Italian country road toward his home in Assisi after an ill-advised battle in Perugia. In truth, to this soldier all battles seemed ill-advised. After such traumatic ordeals, he no longer saw sense to violence or killing.

It was late afternoon, and he was tired and hungry. Ahead he saw a small village. "I'll get something to eat there and find a place for the night," he thought.

Suddenly the horse tripped, throwing the knight to the

ground. He brushed himself off, and saw that the horse had stumbled over a rock jutting out from the roadway. He walked back to the rock, and with the help of his sword, dug the rock out of the ground. It was a splendid rock, almost perfectly round and smooth. The soldier liked the feel of it. So rather than tossing it away he put it in his saddlebags, climbed up on his horse, and continued toward the village.

As he rode past the first houses of the village, people stopped their work to stare. He waved to several of the townsfolk, but no one waved back. Dismounting, the knight approached a woman standing in front of small house. "Good evening," he said cheerfully. "Could you spare a bit of food for an errant knight?"

Sadly, the woman shook her head and sighed, "We've had a poor harvest. There is barely enough for my family. I'm sorry." With these words she walked into the house.

The soldier went to the next house where a farmer was working on his wagon. "Pardon me. Do you have a place at your table for a hungry knight?" he inquired.

"It didn't rain during the last month before harvest," the farmer said. "What little we have is needed to feed our children."

At every home he visited, the knight heard the same sad story: The harvest had been poor. There wasn't enough food to last through the winter; each family needed its grain for seed to plant next year's crop.

Completely discouraged and very hungry, the wandering knight tied his horse to a branch and sat down. "In a few weeks these poor people will be as hungry as I am," he thought. "I pray that I can help them find more food."

An idea flashed in his mind. He reached into his saddlebags, took out the smooth stone and called out to the townsfolk. "Ladies and gentlemen," he shouted, "you are fortunate that I came to your village this day. I have in my possession a special stone that will help feed you through the long winter. With it you can make stone soup."

"Stone soup?" an old woman questioned. "Why I've never heard of such a thing."

"The wonder of stone soup," the soldier explained, "is that it not only feeds hungry people, it helps bring people together. Now who here has a large iron kettle that I can use?"

A large iron pot with a tripod was wheeled out and delivered to the knight. "Now we must fill the pot with water and start a fire," the soldier continued.

Eager hands carried buckets of water and loads of firewood. Soon the pot was hoisted onto a hook over a roaring fire. As the water began to boil, the knight dramatically raised the magic stone above his head and gently placed it into the kettle.

A little boy whispered to his mother, "That stone looks just like the stones we have in our backyard."

The mother picked up her child and assured him. "Hush now! You can't tell if something is magic or special just by looking at the outside."

"You know, I think this stone soup needs some salt and pepper," announced the knight.

Some children hurried to find salt and pepper.

After the water had boiled awhile, the knight tasted the soup. "Umm . . . this stone makes excellent soup, but it would be better if we had a few carrots."

"I have some carrots that I'm willing to share," a farmer replied. Immediately his daughter ran home and returned with an apron filled with carrots.

"It's too bad the harvest was so bad," the knight said sadly. "Stone soup is always more tasty when a cabbage is added."

"Say, I think I know where to find a cabbage or two," a young mother shouted over her shoulder as she ran for home. When she returned she was carrying three large cabbages.

The soldier was busy slicing carrots and cabbages with his sword. "The last time I made stone soup was at the castle of a rich merchant," he said. "The rich merchant added some potatoes and a slab of beef."

Several people quietly talked among themselves. "Hmm . . . a bit of beef and a few potatoes and we can eat like rich people," they whispered. They hurried home and returned not only with beef and potatoes, but also milk, onions, and loaves of bread.

By the time the soup was ready it was dusk. There was an air of excitement as men carted long tables, women brought soup bowls and children carried utensils and cups. It was the most delicious soup the people had ever smelled. And to think it all came from a magic stone brought by a stranger!

After everyone ate their fill, people brought out fiddles and flutes. There was dancing, singing and joy into the early morn. Never had these villagers experienced such a wonderful party.

The next day the entire village gathered to say goodbye to their new friend. "Tell us," a small child asked, "what's your name?"

The knight from Assisi said, "Francis is my name."

As he mounted his horse another child cried out, "Hey, you're forgetting your magic stone."

"Oh I didn't forget," Francis said. "I'm leaving the stone as a gift to the village. Remember me and remember the stone soup," the knight smiled.

It is written in the Book of the Ages that even to this day, no one in that village has ever gone hungry. Nor, in fact, has any villager ever been in want or in need ever since the day the errant knight, Francis of Assisi, stopped by their village and taught them the magic of stone soup.

32.
Garden of the Mind

James Allen

James Allen, in *As A Man Thinketh*, writes, "A man's mind may be likened to a garden, which may be intelligently cultivated or allowed to run wild; but whether cultivated or neglected, it must, and will, bring forth. If no useful seeds are *put* into it, then an abundance of useless weed seeds will *fall* therein, and will continue to produce their own kind."

Allen continues, "Just as a gardener cultivates his plot, keeping it free from weeds, and growing the flowers and fruits, which he requires, so may a man tend the garden of his mind, weeding out all the wrong, useless, and impure thoughts, and cultivating toward perfection the flowers and fruits of right, useful, and pure thoughts. By pursuing this process, a man sooner or later discovers that he is the master gardener of his soul, the director of his life. He also reveals, within himself, the laws of thought, and understands, with ever increasing accuracy, how the thought-forces and mind-elements operate in shaping his character, circumstances, and destiny."

33.
Kindness Wins More Fans

Anonymous

Do you remember Bob Beaman, world record holder in the long jump at the Olympic Games of 1968? Time blurs the memory of even the great feats in athletic history.

Beaman was featured in a commercial promoting the 1984 Summer Olympic Games. In the commercial, he turned to the camera and said, "Back in the Olympic Games of 1968, I set a world record in the long jump. At the time, some people said no one would ever jump that far again. Over the years I've enjoyed watching them try, and I'm told who might have a chance of breaking my record. Well, there's just one thing I have to say about that . . ."

Instead of a self-centered wisecrack, Beaman's face softened, and in a sincere, caring manner, he said, "I hope you make it, kid!"

Bob Beaman won more goodwill with that one act of

kindness than he had ever won with his incredible long jump record of 29 feet, 2 1/2 inches.

34.
"Post-It Notes" Story

Anonymous

There is an interesting story about turning failure into success by recognizing opportunity when it appears. The 3M Company encourages creativity from its employees, allowing its researchers to spend 15% of their time on any project that sparks their interest. This attitude has brought fantastic benefits not only to the employees, but to the company itself. Many times, a spark of an idea, which turned into a successful product, tremendously boosted 3M's corporate profits.

As the story goes, a scientist in 3M's commercial office took advantage of this time for creative thinking. The scientist, Art Fry, sang in his church choir. After marking the appropriate pages in the hymnal by inserting small bits of paper, invariably, the small pieces would fall out on the floor, losing his place.

One day, an inspiration came to Fry. He remembered an adhesive developed by Spencer Silver, a 3M colleague, that everyone considered a failure because it did not stick very well. Fry recalls, "I coated the adhesive on a paper sample and discovered that it was not only a good bookmark, but it was also good for writing notes on it." He continues, "It will stay in place as long as you want, and you can take it off without it sticking to or damaging the page. Then, it can be re-stuck to another page, over and over again."

Yes, Art Fry hit the jackpot. The resulting product was called *Post-It Notes*, and has become one of 3M's most successful products. What was once considered a failure by many became a success because one person's creative thinking recognized a new opportunity. You know, I've often wondered how we ever lived without Post-It Notes.

35.
Wranglers vs. Stranglers

Ted Engstrom

Years ago there was a group of brilliant young men at a midwestern university, who seemed to have amazing, creative literary talent. They were would-be poets, novelists, and essayists. They were extraordinary in their ability to put the English language to its best use. These promising young men met regularly to read and critique each other's work. And critique it they did!

These men were merciless with one another. They dissected the smallest literary expression into a hundred pieces. They were heartless, tough, even mean in their criticism, but they thought they were bringing out each other's best work. Their sessions became such arenas of literary criticism that the members of this exclusive support group nicknamed themselves "The Stranglers."

Not to be outdone, the university's women of literary talent were determined to start a support group of their own, one comparable to "The Stranglers." They called themselves "The Wranglers." They, too, read their works to one another, but there was one significant difference between the two groups. The criticism of "The Wranglers" was much softer, more positive, more encouraging. In fact sometimes there was almost no criticism at all. Every effort, even the most feeble attempt, was gleaned for some bit to be praised and encouraged.

Twenty years later, the university's alumni office was doing an exhaustive study on the careers of its alumni, when it was noticed that there was a great difference in the literary accomplishments of "The Stranglers" as opposed to "The Wranglers." Of all the bright and talented young men in "The Stranglers," not one had made a significant literary accomplishment of any kind. From "The Wranglers" had come six or more successful writers, some attaining national reputation.

Talent between the two? Probably the same. Level of education? Not much difference. But "The Stranglers" strangled, while "The Wranglers" were determined to give each other a boost. "The Stranglers" created an atmosphere of contention and self-doubt. "The Wranglers" highlighted the best, not the worst.

36.
St. Francis de Sales Visits Rome

Anonymous

On one of his visits to Rome, St. Francis de Sales rented two rooms, one for himself and one for his servant, in a small hotel on the banks of the Tiber River. When he returned to the hotel after a long day of business, Francis found his servant arguing with the hotel manager, who wanted to rent out their rooms to someone else at a higher rate.

Francis told his servant, "No quarreling. Come, we'll find other quarters for the night." At such a late hour and with some difficulty, they managed to find rooms, just in time to get out of a torrential rainstorm. The rains fell so heavily that the Tiber overflowed its banks, sweeping away several houses, among them the same hotel where the saint and his servant had stayed previously.

37.
Tame the Wildness

Anonymous

In the old days out West, ranchers would sometimes take a wild horse that they could not break, tie it to a little burro, and turn the two loose. The horse would rear up on its hind legs, snorting defiance, and off they would gallop out on the range.

Before long the bucking steed would disappear over the distant horizon, dragging the helpless burro along. Days would pass, but eventually the odd couple would reappear. The little burro would come first, with the submissive horse in tow.

What happened out on the range always brought the same result. The horse would continue to buck and kick, toss and turn, but the burro, willingly or not, would hang on. Finally, the horse would become exhausted, and at that point the burro would take over, become the leader and lead the way home.

38.
Survival from a Gulag

Anonymous

There was a priest who had been imprisoned in a Russian gulag for a number of years. Finally, in the early 1970s, he was released from prison and exiled to England.

Shortly after arriving, he met with reporters and was asked how he was able to survive all those years in the gulag. Thoughtfully, the priest responded that he felt his survival was much like that of the oak tree which stood in a nearby field. He related, "I guess I'm just another nut who wouldn't give up."

39.
Still Rope, Still Hope

Anonymous

A story is told about an oilman who started to drill a new well on his land. In oil field jargon, the drilling pipe is called a "rope."

After drilling a deep hole, there was no oil to be found. The owner decided that it was a dead hole, and told the crew boss to cap the well. He would write it off as a complete loss.

Meanwhile, the foreman called to the driller and asked how much "rope" was left on the rig. "About six to eight feet," replied the driller.

"Then keep on drilling deeper," shouted the foreman.

After drilling only two feet more, the well struck oil, and was one of the most productive wells in the entire oil field.

We can learn a lot about life from the drilling of an oil well; while there is still rope, there is still room for hope.

40.
A Different Vision

Joseph Girzone

Each person looks at life with a different vision. Three persons can look at a tree. One will see so many board feet of valuable lumber worth so much money. The second one will see it as so much firewood to be burned to keep one's family warm in the winter. The third will see it as a masterpiece of God's creative art, given to people as an expression of God's love and enduring strength. It has a value far beyond its worth in money or firewood.

What we live for determines what we see in life and gives clearer focus to our inner vision.

41.
Never Lose Sight of Goals

Anonymous

The California coast was blanketed in fog July 4, 1952. Twenty-one miles to the west, on Catalina Island, Florence

Chadwick, a 34-year-old long-distance swimmer, waded in to the water and began swimming toward the California coast. She had already conquered the English Channel, swimming in both directions. Now she was determined to be the first woman to swim the Catalina Channel.

As the hours ticked off, Chadwick fought bone-chilling cold, dense fog, and sharks. Several times, sharks had to be driven off by rifles. Fatigue never set in, but the icy water numbed her to the point of exhaustion. Straining to make out the shore through her swimmer's goggles, she could see only dense fog. She knew she could not go any farther. Although not a quitter, Chadwick shouted to her trainer and her mother in the boat and asked to be taken out of the water. They urged her not to give up, but when she looked toward the California coast, all she could see was thick fog.

So after fifteen hours and fifty-five minutes of fighting the elements, she was hauled from the channel into the boat. Frozen to the bone and her spirit defeated, Chadwick was devastated when she discovered that she was only a half mile from the coast! She felt the shock of failure. "Look, I'm not excusing myself," she told a reporter, "but if I could have seen land, I know I could have made it." She had been licked not by fatigue or even by the cold. The fog alone had defeated her because it had obscured her goal. It had blinded her reason, her eyes, and most of all, her heart.

Two months later, Chadwick swam that same channel, and again fog clouded her vision, but this time she swam with her faith intact—that somewhere behind that fog was land. This time she succeeded. Not only was she the first woman to swim the Catalina Channel, but she beat the men's record by two hours.

42.
Good News Report
Anonymous

An executive did an amazing job of transforming a run-down office into an outstanding success. Her secret was to request each department head to submit a weekly report each Monday morning of all the good things that had happened in their departments during the preceding week. This was a simple enough way to turn a failed organization into a dynamic success.

43.
Shortcuts in Life

Zig Ziglar

Zig Ziglar tells a story about a man named Emmanuel Ninnger who in the 1880s paid for his weekly groceries with a twenty dollar bill. The clerk counted out the change and Ninnger left the store. The clerk then noticed smudges on her sweaty hands. She picked up the twenty and noticed smudges on it, too, which she then showed to the store manager.

The manager called the police who identified the bill as being counterfeit. In fact, the officer said it was a masterful piece of counterfeiting. Detectives got a warrant for Ninnger's apartment, and in their investigation, discovered an easel near the window to which was clipped a genuine twenty dollar bill. Amazing as it sounds, what Ninnger did was painstakingly handpaint each separate twenty dollar bill, one at a time. They were near perfect copies.

Continuing the search, in an attic workroom the police discovered three discarded portraits previously painted by Ninnger which when sold at auction fetched over $5,000 apiece.

The ironic part of this story is that it took Emmanuel Ninnger about the same time to paint a $5,000 portrait as it took to handpaint a twenty dollar bill.

Emmanuel Ninnger was quite a thief, and probably would not have been caught except for a grocery clerk with sweaty palms. But from whom did Ninnger steal most? From none other than Emmanuel Ninnger himself.

Trying to take shortcuts in life is only stealing from yourself. Are you utilizing your abilities to their fullest potential, or are you stealing from yourself?

44.
Earthy Mysticism

John Donne

John Donne, a 17th century English poet, wrote a story about one man's search for God.

The man is told that God lives atop a high mountain at the end of the earth. After a long journey, the man arrives at the mountain and begins his climb.

About the time that the man begins his ascent, God muses, "What can I do to show my people how much I love them?" God gets the idea to descend the mountain and live among his people as one of them.

And so as the man is ascending one side of the mountain, God is descending the other side. However, they don't see each other because they are on opposite sides of the mountain. When the man reaches the mountaintop, he is heartbroken to find no one there. He thinks, "God doesn't live here after all." He even begins to think that God doesn't exist, saying, "If God doesn't live here, where does God live?"

Donne concludes, "God doesn't dwell on mountaintops, or in the midst of the desert, or at the ends of the earth. God dwells with men and women. God lives in the towns and cities of the world."

45.
A Short-Sighted Bishop

Anonymous

In 1870, a bishop expressed to the president of a small denominational college his short-sighted, but firm, biblical conviction that nothing new could be invented. The educator disagreed and believed there was much left to be discovered. "Why, I believe it may even be possible for people in the future to fly through the air like a bird," said the college president.

The bishop was aghast. "Flying is reserved for the angels," he insisted. "I beg you not to mention that again, lest you be guilty of blasphemy!" That narrow-minded bishop immediately left with his two sons, Orville and Wilbur.

Only thirty-three years later the Wright Brothers, Orville and Wilbur, made their first flight in a heavier-than-air machine, which was the precursor of the airplane.

How wrong you were, Bishop Wright! How open are you to the possibility of new ideas, new discoveries?

46.
The Beatitudes: The Lesson

Anonymous

Jesus took his disciples up the mountain, gathered them around him and began to teach them saying:

"Blessed are the poor in spirit for theirs is the kingdom
of heaven.
Blessed are the meek.
Blessed are they who mourn.
Blessed are the merciful.
Blessed are they who thirst for justice.
Blessed are you when persecuted.
Blessed are you when you suffer.
Be glad and rejoice for your reward will be great in
heaven . . ."

Simon Peter spoke up and said, "Do we have to write this stuff down?" Andrew asked, "Are we supposed to remember this?" James piped in, "Will we be tested on this?" Philip asked, "What if we don't understand it?" Bartholomew inquired, "Is this an assignment to turn in?" John said, "The other disciples didn't have to learn all this." Matthew said, "When do we get off this mountain?" And Judas questioned, "What does this have to do with real life anyway?"

Then one of the Pharisees present asked to see Jesus' lesson plans. Another demanded to know Jesus' terminal objectives in the cognitive domain . . .

And Jesus wept!

47.
Compassion Is in the Eyes

Anonymous

It was a bitter, cold evening in northern Virginia many years ago. The old man's beard was glazed by winter's frost while he waited for a ride across the river. The wait seemed endless. His body became numb and stiff from the frigid north wind.

He heard the faint, steady rhythm of approaching hooves galloping along the frozen path. Anxiously, he watched as several horsemen rounded the bend. He let the first one pass by without an effort to get his attention. Then another passed by, and another. Finally, the last rider neared the spot where the old man sat like a snow statue. As this one drew near, the old man caught the rider's eye and said, "Sir, would you mind giving an old man a ride to the other side? There doesn't appear to be a passageway by foot."

Reining his horse, the rider replied, "Sure thing. Hop aboard." Seeing the old man was unable to lift his half-frozen body from the ground, the horseman dismounted and helped the old man onto the horse. The horseman took the old man not just across the river, but to his destination, which was just a few miles away. As they neared the tiny, but cozy cottage, the horseman's curiosity caused him to inquire, "Sir, I notice that you let several other riders pass by without making an effort to secure a ride. Then I come up and you immediately asked me for a ride. I'm curious why, on such a bitter winter night, you would wait and ask the last rider. What if I had refused and left you there?"

The old man lowered himself slowly down from the horse, looked the rider straight in the eyes, and replied, "I've been around these here parts for some time. I reckon I know people pretty good." The old-timer continued, "I looked into the eyes of the other riders and immediately saw there was no concern for my situation. It would have been useless even to ask them for a ride. But when I looked into your eyes, kindness and compassion were evident. I knew, then and there, that your gentle spirit would welcome the opportunity to give me assistance in my time of need."

Those heartwarming comments touched the horseman deeply. "I'm most grateful for what you have said," he told the old man. "May I never get too busy in my own affairs that I fail to respond to the needs of others with kindness and compassion."

With that, Thomas Jefferson turned his horse around and made his way back to the White House.

48.
God Who Enables

Faye Sweeney

"It is God who enables you
to smile in spite of tears;
to carry on when you feel like giving in;
to pray when you're at a loss for words;
to love even though your heart has been broken time
    and time again;

to sit calmly when you feel like throwing up your
    hands in frustration;
to be understanding when nothing seems to make
    sense;
to listen when you'd really rather not hear;
to share your feelings with others, because sharing is
    necessary to ease the load.

Anything is possible,
because God makes it so."

49.
The Clump of Grass

Brian Cavanaugh, T.O.R.

A story is told about a village on a South Pacific Island
where a missionary made his monthly visit to celebrate the
Mass, baptize children and new initiates, witness marriage
vows, anoint the sick and pray for the recently deceased. In
this particular village a unique custom is practiced whenever
the missionary arrives in his seaplane.

By tradition, the village chief is the first to greet the padre
when he steps on land. The two of them embrace, then the
chieftain gives the priest a clump of dune grass. The priest
returns the clump of grass to the chief, who then turns and
gives it to the person next to him. According to island custom,
the clump of earth and grass is a sacred reminder of God's
presence to the people who live with the vast ocean about
them. The islanders consider it a type of sacramental symboliz-
ing harmony and peace.

This sacred clump of grass passes from one villager to the
next, throughout the entire village, until it returns to the chief,
who then presents it to the priest, completing the ritual. The
custom with the sacred clump of grass symbolizes that the
villagers are in harmony with one another and are at peace. It
is at this point that the Mass can begin, and not before.

On this particular visit the padre went about his other duties as usual. When the customary time neared for the joyous celebration of the Eucharist, word came to the priest that there was going to be a delay. It seems that there was a bitter disagreement between a father and son, and the clump of grass had not been exchanged between them. There was no celebration of the Mass that month nor the next. It took three months before harmony and peace was restored to that family and to the island village.

As I reflect on this story, I see the beauty and sacredness of that South Pacific custom. I wonder what would happen if we were to pass a sacred clump of grass throughout our churches before we began the Eucharistic celebration. Would there be harmony and peace? How long would we have to wait before we celebrated the Liturgy of the Eucharist?

50.
A Ton of Bricks

Brian Cavanaugh, T.O.R.

I recently remembered a personal experience which brought back uneasy feelings of frustration and impending crisis. I remembered that it felt as if a "ton of bricks" was being dropped on me in that moment.

In my reflections, I considered the following question, "What do you do when someone drops on you what seems to be a ton of bricks?" I envisioned both negative and positive responses to such a situation.

The pile of bricks can be used to build a wall, a fort, or even a tomb, wherein a person can attempt to isolate and protect oneself.

Or the same "ton of bricks" can be used to build a bridge, a ramp, or a passageway into a future of renewed life and freedom.

Which will be your response if the proverbial "ton of bricks" lands on you?

51.
Obstacle or Opportunity

Anonymous

In ancient times, a king had a huge boulder placed in a roadway, then he hid and watched to see if anyone would remove it. Some of the kingdom's wealthiest merchants and courtiers came by and simply walked around it. Many of them loudly blamed the king for not keeping the roads clear, but none of them did anything about getting the big stone out of the way.

Then a peasant farmer came along, carrying a load of vegetables on his back. When he came to the boulder, he laid down his burden and began trying to move the stone to the side of the road. After much pushing and straining, he finally succeeded.

As he picked up his load of vegetables, he noticed a purse lying in the road where the boulder had been. The purse contained many gold coins and a note from the king indicating that the gold was for the person who removed the boulder from the roadway.

The peasant learned what many others have learned since: Every obstacle presents an opportunity to improve one's condition.

52.
It's in Your Hands

Anonymous

High on a hilltop overlooking the beautiful city of Santa Barbara there lived a wise old man whom people considered a sage. Legend has it that he could answer any question posed to him.

Two local boys decided they could deceive the old man and trip him up. Figuring they had a plan that was foolproof, the boys caught a small bird and headed for the mountaintop. As they approached the sage, one of the boys cupped the bird in his hands, which he held behind his back.

"Wise old man," he posed, "can you tell me if this bird in my hands is alive or dead?"

The old man sized up the two boys, and without hesitation, answered. "My boy, if I tell you that the bird is alive, you will close your hands and crush the bird to death. And if I say that the bird is dead, you will open your hands and let it fly away." He continued, "You see, boy, in your hands you hold the power over life and death. And it's an awesome responsibility."

The boys were stunned. They glanced at one another in total amazement. This old man truly is wise, very wise, they thought. They had not fooled him for one minute. The old man stroked his long white beard, smiled gently and looked them square in the eyes. He said, "This I say to both of you without qualification," he explained in a sincere voice. "In your hands you hold the seeds of failure, or the potential for success. Your hands are very capable, but they must be used for the right things. They must be used to reap rewards that you are capable of attaining."

As the bewildered boys descended back down the mountain, the wind of a new attitude swirled about them, and they eagerly freed the captive bird. They watched the bird flap its wings and followed its spiraling flight of freedom. It was in that moment that the boys understood just how precious the old master's advice was.

53.
The Traveler and the Shepherd

Anonymous

A traveler was returning to his home from a journey to a distant country. At nightfall he arrived at the entrance to a vast forest. Unable either to delay his journey or retrace his steps, he was prepared to traverse the sullen forest when he came upon an old shepherd from whom he asked the way.

"Alas!" cried the shepherd. "It is not easy to point it out, for the forest is criss-crossed by hundreds of paths winding in every direction. They are almost all similar in appearance, though all with one exception lead to the Great Abyss."

"What is the Great Abyss?" the traveler inquired.

"It is the abyss which surrounds the forest," replied the shepherd. "Moreover, the forest is filled with robbers and wild beasts. In particular, it is ravaged by an enormous serpent, so that scarcely a day passes but we find the remains of some unfortunate traveler who fell prey to it. Still," the shepherd continued, "as it is impossible to arrive at the place where you are going without traversing the forest, I have, through a motive of compassion, stationed myself at the entrance of the forest to assist and direct travelers. I have also placed my sons at different intervals to assist me in the same good work. Their services and mine are at your disposal, and I am ready to accompany you if you so desire."

The candor and venerable appearance of the old man satisfied the traveler, and he accepted the proposal. The shepherd held a lantern with one hand and with the other took the arm of the traveler. They then set out upon their journey through the dark forest.

After walking for some distance, the traveler felt his strength waning. "Lean on me," said the shepherd. The traveler did so, and was able to continue the journey. At length the lamp began to flicker.

"Ah!" groaned the traveler. "The oil is nearly spent, and the light will soon be gone. What will become of us now?"

"Do not fear," consoled the shepherd. "We shall soon meet one of my sons, who will supply us with more oil." Just then the traveler perceived a glimmer of light shining through the darkness. The light shone from a small cabin by the side of the narrow path. At the sound of the shepherd's well-known voice, the cabin door swung open. A seat was offered to the weary traveler, and some plain but substantial food was set before him. Thus refreshed, the traveler set out again, guided by the shepherd's son.

In this manner the traveler journeyed on for the rest of the night. From time to time, they stopped at different cabins built along the path. At each stop he obtained refreshment, a bit of rest and was furnished with a new guide. With the dawning of daylight, the traveler arrived, without incident, at the farthest boundary of the forest. Only then did he appreciate the magnitude of the service rendered him by the shepherd and his sons. At the very edge of the forest, right before his feet, lay a frightful precipice, at the bottom of which he could distinguish the roar of an angry current.

"This," said his guide, "is the Great Abyss which my father spoke about. No one knows its depth, for it is always covered with a thick fog which no eye can penetrate."

As he spoke, he heaved a deep sigh, and wiped a tear from his eyes. "You seem grieved," said the traveler.

"How can it be otherwise?" replied his guide. "Can I look at the abyss without thinking of the thousands of unfortunate people who every day are swallowed up in it? In vain do my father and my brothers offer our services. Very few accept them, and of those few the greater portion, after journeying for a few hours, accuse us of needlessly alarming them. They despise our advice and set out on paths of their own choosing. The consequence is that they soon lose their way and are devoured by the serpent, murdered by robbers, or plunge headlong into the abyss. You see there is only this one little bridge by which the Great Abyss can be crossed, and the way which leads to the bridge is known to us alone. Pass over with confidence," continued the guide. He turned to the traveler, embraced him and said, "On the other side is your true home."

The traveler, overcome with gratitude, thanked his charitable guide and promised never to forget him. He crossed the narrow bridge and discovered he was now in his own land. His family was there to welcome him.

54.
Only Cheating Yourself

Anonymous

A young carpenter married a building contractor's daughter. Soon thereafter, the father-in-law decided to boost the career of his new son-in-law.

"Son," he said, "I don't want you to start at the bottom of this construction business as I did. I want you to go out to my job-site and build the most tremendous house this town has ever seen. Put the best of everything in it, make it a showplace, and turn it over to me when you are finished."

"Well, this is an opportunity to make a killing," thought the son-in-law. He hurried out to slap together a building that would survive two fairly stiff gales. He made a deal with a shady wholesaler and installed sub-standard lumber, shingles, cinder blocks, cement, etc., but billed for the "best" materials. The two cheats split the profits from their deception. In short order the son-in-law presented his father-in-law with the keys to the newly finished house.

"Is it a tremendous showplace of the newest and best materials as I asked?" inquired the father-in-law.

"It sure is, dad," answered the son-in-law.

"Is it the finest house ever built, son?"

"You betcha, dad."

"All right, where's the final bill? And did you include a good profit in it for yourself?"

"Uh, well. . . . Here it is," the son-in-law replied, "and yes, I did."

"OK. Let me write out a check. Do you have the deed with you?"

As he accepted the deed, the father-in-law said, "I didn't tell you why I wanted that house to be the best ever built. I wanted it to be something special that I could give to you and my daughter to show you how much I love you. Here, take the deed and the keys. Go live in that showplace; it's yours now. Go live in the house you built—*for yourself*!"

The young man slinked away, shattered and frustrated. He thought he was making a fortune at his father-in-law's expense by shaving money here and there with inferior materials and various shortcuts, but in the end he only cheated himself.

55.
Public Speaking Qualifications

Anonymous

President Dwight Eisenhower, speaking at the National Press Club, told the audience that he regretted he was not much of an orator. "It reminds me of my boyhood days on a Kansas farm," he related. "An old farmer had a dairy cow we wanted to buy. My dad and I went over to ask him about the cow's pedigree. The old farmer didn't know what pedigree meant. So my dad asked him about the cow's butterfat production. He told us that he hadn't any idea what that was either. Finally, dad asked him if he knew how many pounds of milk the cow produced each year.

"By now that old farmer was puzzled. He shook his head and said, 'I don't know. But one thing I do know for sure is that she's an honest old cow, and she'll give you all the milk she has!' "

"Well," Eisenhower concluded, "I'm like that old cow. I'll give you everything I have (as president)."

Though he was not highly regarded as a speech maker, President Eisenhower gave the United States of America everything he had. The freedom we enjoy today bears witness to his ability.

56.
Letter to Diogentus

Anonymous, 2nd century A.D.

Christians are not differentiated from other people by country, language or customs. You see, they do not live in cities of their own, or speak some strange dialect, or have some peculiar lifestyle. Their teachings have not been contrived by the invention and speculation of inquisitive individuals; nor are Christians promulgating mere human teaching as some people do. They live in both Greek and foreign cities, wherever chance has put them. They follow local customs in clothing, food and the other necessities of life. But at the same time, they demonstrate to us the wonderful and certainly unusual form of their own citizenship.

They live in their own native lands, but as aliens. As citizens, they share all things with others, but like aliens they suffer all things. Every foreign country is to them like their native country, and every native land like a foreign country. They marry and have children just like everyone else; but they do not kill unwanted babies. They offer a shared table, but not a shared bed. They are at present "in the flesh," but they do not live "according to the flesh." They are passing their days on earth, but are citizens of heaven. They obey the appointed laws, and go beyond the laws in their own lives.

They love everyone, but are persecuted by all. They are

unknown and condemned; they are put to death and gain life. They are poor and yet make many rich. They are short of everything and yet have plenty of all things. They are dishonored and yet gain glory through dishonor. Their names are blackened and yet they are cleared. They are mocked and they bless in return. They are treated outrageously and behave respectfully to others. When they do good, they are punished as evildoers. When punished, they rejoice as if being given new life. They are attacked as aliens and are persecuted; yet those who hate them cannot give any reason for their hostility.

To put it simply, the soul is to the body as Christians are to the world. The soul is spread through all parts of the body, and Christians through all the cities of the world. The soul is in the body but is not of the body. Christians are in the world but not of the world.

57.
Lives Out of Balance

Anonymous

In 1923, nine of the world's most successful financiers met at Chicago's Edgewater Beach Hotel. Financially, they literally "held the world by the tail." Anything that money could buy was within their grasp; they were rich—rich—rich! Read their names and the high position each held:

1. Charles Schwab, president of the largest steel company;
2. Samuel Insull, president of the largest electric utility company;
3. Howard Hopson, president of the largest gas company;
4. Arthur Cutten, the great wheat speculator;
5. Richard Whitney, president of the New York Stock Exchange;

6. Albert Fall, Secretary of Interior in President Harding's Cabinet;
7. Leon Fraser, president of the Bank of International Settlements;
8. Jesse Livermore, greatest "bear" on Wall Street;
9. Ivar Kreuger, head of the world's greatest monopoly.

Certainly we must admit that here were gathered a group of the world's most successful men—at least, men who had found the secret of making money. Let's see where these men were 25 years later, in 1948:

1. the president of the largest independent steel company, Charles Schwab died bankrupt and lived on borrowed money for five years before his death;

2. the president of the largest utility company, Samuel Insull died a fugitive from justice and penniless in a foreign land;

3. the president of the largest gas company, Howard Hopson was insane;

4. the great wheat speculator, Arthur Cutten died abroad—insolvent;

5. the president of the New York Stock Exchange, Richard Whitney was released from Sing Sing Penitentiary;

6. the member of the president's cabinet, Albert Fall was pardoned from prison so he could die at home—broke;

7. the president of the Bank of International Settlements, Leon Fraser died a suicide;

8. the "great bear" of Wall Street, Jesse Livermore committed suicide;

9. Ivar Kreuger, the great monopoly player, also took his own life.

All these men learned well the art of making money, but not one of them learned how to live. A vast amount of talent and potential went down the drain with these men.

What happened? Their lives were out of balance!

58.
The Origins of the Christmas Crib
From The Life of St. Francis (*Legenda Maior*)

by
St. Bonaventure

It happened in the third year before his death that St. Francis decided, in order to arouse devotion, to celebrate at Greccio with the greatest possible solemnity the memory of the birth of the Child Jesus. So that this would not be considered a type of novelty, he petitioned for and obtained permission from the Supreme Pontiff. He had a crib prepared, hay carried in and an ox and an ass led to the place. The friars are summoned, the people come, the forest resounds with their voices and that venerable night is rendered brilliant and solemn by a multitude of bright lights and by resonant and harmonious hymns of praise. The man of God stands before the crib, filled with affection, bathed in tears and overflowing with joy. A solemn Mass is celebrated over the crib, with Francis as deacon chanting the holy Gospel. Then he preaches to the people standing about concerning the birth of the poor King, whom, when he wished to name him, he called in his tender love, the Child of Bethlehem.

A certain virtuous and truthful knight, Sir John of Greccio, who had abandoned worldly military activity out of love of Christ and had become an intimate friend of the man of God, claimed that he saw a beautiful little boy asleep in the crib and that the blessed father Francis embraced it in both of his arms and seemed to wake it from sleep.

Not only does the holiness of the witness
make credible
this vision of the devout knight,
but also the truth it expresses
proves its validity
and the subsequent miracles confirm it.
For Francis' example
when considered by the world
is capable of arousing
the hearts of those who are sluggish
in the faith of Christ.

The hay from the crib
was kept by the people
and miraculously cured sick animals
and drove away different kinds of pestilence.
Thus God glorified his servant in every way
and demonstrated the efficacy
of his holy prayer
by the evident signs
of wonderful miracles.

59.
A Simple Gesture

Anonymous

History was made in the baseball world in 1947. It was
in that year that Jackie Robinson became the first black player
in the major leagues. The Brooklyn Dodgers' owner, Branch
Rickey, told Robinson, "It'll be tough on you. You are going
to take a lot of abuse, be ridiculed, and receive more verbal
punishment than you ever thought possible." Rickey continued, "But I'm willing to back you all the way if you have the
determination to make it work."

In short order, Robinson experienced Rickey's gloomy

prediction. He was abused verbally and physically as players intentionally ran him over and ran him down. The crowd was quick with racial slurs and deriding comments. Opponents, as well as his own teammates, ridiculed Robinson.

Around mid-season, Robinson was having a particularly horrendous day. He had fumbled several grounders, over-thrown first base, and batted poorly. The crowd that day was especially nasty. Then something miraculous happened. In front of this critical crowd, Pee Wee Reese, the team captain, walked over from his shortstop position and put his arm around Jackie Robinson.

Robinson later reflected, "That simple gesture saved my career. Pee Wee made me feel as if I belonged."

60.
Lost Island Legend

Brian Cavanaugh, T.O.R.

According to an ancient legend from the South Seas, a sudden, ferocious storm blew up in the darkest part of the night catching a sailing ship in its grip. The crashing waves and lashing wind ripped into wood and canvas tearing the ship asunder. The crew struggled to grab onto whatever would float, hoping they would not slip beneath the frothing sea that night.

With the dawning sun the survivors saw a not-too-distant island. They paddled and swam to the island as best they could, collapsing on the beach exhausted and frightened, but alive. After several hours, they awoke and oriented themselves to their circumstances. They wondered where they were, for this island did not appear on any of their charts. Did the storm blow them far off course? The survivors decided that the first thing they needed to do was scavenge the wreckage for fire-wood and materials with which to construct shelters. By night-fall they had scrounged materials to build simple shelters, found a little food and gathered enough wood to build a large signal fire should a passing ship be sighted. Tired and fatigued, they huddled around the safety of a small fire, each man telling a harrowing tale of the past twenty-four hours.

Suddenly, the night's stillness was broken by noises from the forest. A band of armed natives emerged from the brush and surrounded the terrified sailors. The leader of the natives moved toward the group with his palms outward as a sign of peace. He motioned and gestured that the sailors were to come with him to his village where they would be looked after. But when the native leader got closer and was within the firelight, the survivors were more frightened than before.

The native had no eyes. It wasn't that he was blind, or had lost his eyes, he simply was without eyes or even openings of where eyes should be. Looking around them, the sailors noticed the appearance of the other natives. Their faces had no eyes as well.

The native leader sensed their fear and tried to communicate through signs and gestures that it was not safe to stay on the beach, and that they should follow him to his village. The natives led the way through the brush until they came to a trail that wound its way up the mountain to the safety of their village. The shipwrecked survivors bumped, stumbled and crawled through tortuous and hazardous terrain. They grumbled among themselves, "I don't get it. How is it that these natives with no eyes can move so quickly and at night, when we're hitting this or stumbling over that?" Finally the sounds of the village reached their ears. They felt an end to their grueling journey was within reach.

However, on entering the village the sailors were unsettled further when they noticed that no one in the village had eyes. In fact, the entire tribe had no eyes. Almost as one they thought, "How can they get around and do things, especially at night and in the dark, without being able to see?"

The leader of the band of natives went to the village chief with his report. The chief listened as his son said, "Father, you were right. The violent storm did cause a shipwreck. We

57

followed these survivors all day listening to determine if they were peaceful, or not. They speak a strange language," the son continued, "so all we could do was use gestures and signs to try and get them to understand that we meant them no harm, and that we would bring them to safety, shelter and food. But, father," the son went on, "I feel such compassion for them. They are very helpless men. Why on the trail coming up the mountain I had to position our people among them because they kept hitting their heads on tree limbs, and stumbling on roots. Two of them nearly fell into a ravine. I don't understand why they couldn't sense those things and feel their way up the mountain. Father, we need to give them all the help we can. They are so helpless."

61.
Heaven or Hell?

Anonymous

Once there was a knight who traveled a long distance to see a sage and asked, "Wise Master, tell me, what are heaven and hell really like?"

"Tell me about yourself first," replied the sage.

"I am an officer of the Emperor's elite personal guard," he answered.

"Nonsense!" the wise man retorted. "What kind of emperor would have you around him? To me you appear like a fool."

The knight was infuriated by such an insult. He reached for his sword. "Oh, ho," exclaimed the sage. "So you have a long sword. I'll bet it's much too dull to cut off my head."

At this, the knight could not hold himself back. He angrily drew his sword and threatened the wise master, who calmly replied, "Now you know half the answer. You are opening the gates of hell."

The officer hesitated, lowered his sword, and bowed in respect. "Now you know the other half," said the sage. "You have opened the gates of heaven."

62.
Toward Self-Destruction

Anonymous

There is a fable that tells about a lion and a tiger. Both thirsty, the animals arrived at the water hole at the same time. They immediately began to argue about which should satisfy its thirst first. The argument became heated. Each one decided it would rather die than give up the privilege of being first to quench its thirst.

Stubbornly they confronted each other, and their emotions turned to rage. However, their vicious attacks on each other were suddenly interrupted. They both looked up toward the sky, and circling overhead was a flock of vultures waiting for the loser to fall. Quietly, the two beasts turned away from each other and withdrew back into the forest. The thought of being devoured was all they needed to end their quarrel.

63.
Be a Lamplighter

Brian Cavanaugh, T.O.R.

Several parents were sitting on a neighbor's porch discussing their children. They were talking about the negative environment in which the kids had to grow up—an environment filled with drugs, violence, and a pervading feeling of hopelessness. How could they, the parents, bring any light into their children's world since it seems so dark and hopeless? Could they be enough of a positive influence in their children's lives that the children would not just survive, but possibly work to change the world around them? The discussion went on for some time.

One of the parents, a science teacher, remarked, "I think we can make a difference in our children's lives if we become lamplighters."

"Lamplighters? What do you mean?" the others asked.

She explained. "Around the turn of the century a lamplighter went around the streets lighting the streetlamps. He carried a long pole that had a small candle on top with which he would reach up to light the kerosene-fed lamps. But from a distance you could not see a lamplighter very well. The light from one small candle was not very bright in the surrounding darkness of night.

"However," she continued, "you could follow the progress of the lamplighter as he went along a street. The presence of his candle was barely visible until it joined with the flame of the streetlamp being newly lit. A radiant glow erased a portion of the night's darkness, and looking back down the street, you could see that the light from the glowing streetlamps made the entire street bright as day. The darkness was held at bay."

Almost as a chorus the parents exclaimed, "That's it! We'll be lamplighters for our children. We'll be their role models. We'll share from our own flame in order to light each child's individual lamp of wisdom, and by our love provide the fuel necessary to nourish and sustain its flame. Then we will have helped them become bright enough themselves so that they can conquer the darkness and hopelessness of their world."

64.
Make a Difference

Anonymous

There is a story told about the late Sam Rayburn, former Speaker for the House of Representatives. One of his friend's daughter was critically injured in a car accident and early the next morning Mr. Rayburn knocked on his friend's front door. "I just came by to see what I could do to help," inquired Rayburn.

The father replied that there was nothing to do.

"Well," Rayburn said, "have you had your morning coffee yet?"

The man said that they had not taken time for breakfast. While Rayburn was working in the kitchen, his friend came in and asked, "Mr. Speaker, I thought you were supposed to be having breakfast at the White House this morning?"

"I was," said Rayburn, "but I called the President and told him I had a friend who was in need and that I couldn't come to the White House."

What a different world this would be if we could learn to become more caring and more unselfish.

65.
Night and Day

Anonymous

Late one night the Teacher sat around a blazing fire with a small number of disciples. Their conversation was broken by periods of silence when they gazed at the stars or stared into the glowing embers. Suddenly the Teacher posed a question: "How can we know when the night has ended and the day has begun?"

Eagerly a young man answered, "You know the night is

61

over when you can look off in the distance and tell which animal is a dog and which is a sheep. Is that the right answer, Teacher?"

"It is a good answer," the Teacher said slowly, "but it isn't quite the answer I would give."

A second disciple ventured a guess. "You know the night is over when the light falls on the leaves and you can tell whether it is an olive tree or a fig tree," she said.

Once again the Teacher shook his head. "That was a fine answer; still, it is not the answer I seek," he said gently.

Immediately the disciples began to argue with one another. Finally, one of them begged the Teacher, "Answer your own question, Teacher, for we cannot think of another response."

The Teacher looked intently at the eager faces before he spoke. "When you look into the eyes of another human being and see a brother or a sister, you will know it is morning. If you cannot see a brother or a sister, you will know that no matter what time it is, for you it will always be night. And you will always be in the dark."

66.
Importance of the Obvious

Anonymous

Calvin Coolidge, 30th President of the United States, was called *Silent Cal* because he was usually brief in speech. However, because he used words sparingly, it did not mean that *Silent Cal* was without wisdom or the ability to articulate a sound idea.

Once, for instance, Coolidge had this to say: "People criticize me for harping on the obvious. Perhaps someday I'll write an article on 'The Importance of the Obvious.'

"If all the folks in the United States would do the few

simple things they know they ought to do, most of our big problems would take care of themselves."

67.
Meaning of Christmas

Anonymous

Once upon a cold Christmas Eve, a man sat in reflective silence before the flames flickering in the fireplace, thinking about the meaning of Christmas. "There is no point to a God who became human," he mused. "Why would an all-powerful God want to share even one of his precious moments with the likes of us? And even if he did, why would God choose to be born in a stable? No way! The whole thing is absurd! I'm sure that if God really wanted to come down to earth, he would have chosen some other way."

Suddenly, the man was roused from his musings by a strange sound outside. He sprang to the window and leaned on the sash. Outside he saw a gaggle of snow geese frantically honking and wildly flapping their wings amid the deep snow and frigid cold. They seemed dazed and confused. Apparently, due to exhaustion, they had dropped out of a larger flock migrating to a warmer climate.

Moved to compassion, the man bundled up and went outside. He tried to "shoo" the shivering geese into the warm garage, but the more he "shooed," the more the geese panicked. "If they only realized that I'm trying to save them," he thought to himself. "How can I make them understand my concern for their well-being?"

Then a thought came to him: "If for just a minute, I could become one of them, if I could become a snow goose and communicate with them in their own language, then they would know what I'm trying to do."

In a flash of inspiration, he remembered it was Christmas Eve. A warm smile crossed his face. The Christmas story no longer seemed absurd. He visualized an ordinary-looking infant lying in a manger in a stable in Bethlehem. He understood the answer to his Christmas problem: God became one-like-us to tell us, in human terms, that we can understand, that he loves us, that he loves us right now, and that he is concerned with our well-being.

68.
Secret of Success (adapted)

Clarence DeLoach, Jr.

A successful businessman once was asked for the secret of success by a student who interviewed him as part of his senior thesis. Thoughtfully, the businessman pondered the question. His reply summed up success in three words: *"and then some."* "You see," he said, "I learned early in life that the difference between average people and the truly successful could be simply stated in those three words. Top people did what was expected, *and then some!"*

The truly successful were thoughtful of others; they were considerate and kind—*and then some.* They met their obligations and responsibilities fairly and squarely—*and then some.* They were good friends and helpful neighbors—*and then some.* They could be counted on in an emergency—*and then some.*

Jesus taught the *and then some* principle in the Sermon on the Mount. He tells us to go beyond what is expected! Go a little bit farther!

Let the words, *"and then some,"* serve as a tonic for your spirit. Practice your faith faithfully—*and then some.* Give generously of your time and of your resources—*and then some.* Greet those you meet with a smile—*and then some.* Be dependable, be a good friend—*and then some.* Do your best in all things and at all times—*and then some.* Be among the truly successful who go the extra mile, who make the world more livable and demonstrate true caring for the people around them—*and then some.*

69.
Rating Code for Sermons

Anonymous

Recently I came across an item titled "Rating Code for Sermons" that made me stop to think about my preaching. See if it has anything to say to you.

"G" = Generally acceptable to everyone. Full of inoffensive, puerile platitudes. Usually described as "wonderful" or "marvelous."

"PG" = For more mature congregations. At times this sermon makes the Gospel relevant to today's issues. May even contain mild suggestions for change. Often described as "challenging," though no one intends to take any action or change any attitudes.

"R" = Definitely restricted to those not upset by truth. This sermon "tells it like it is." Threatens the comfortable; most often described as "disturbing" or "controversial." Usually indicates that the preacher has an outside source of income.

"X" = Positively limited to those who can handle bombshell/explosive ideas. This sermon really "socks it to 'em." The kind of sermon that landed Jeremiah in the well, got Amos run out of town, surprised Jonah, and nailed Jesus to the cross. Always described as "shocking" or "in poor taste." The minister who preaches this sermon had better have his/her suitcase packed and life insurance paid in full.

70.
The Weight of a Snowflake (adapted)

Anonymous

Not too long ago in a place not too far away, a field mouse asked a wise old owl what is the weight of a snowflake. "Why nothing more than nothing," answered the owl.

The mouse went on to tell the owl about the time he was resting on a branch in a fir tree, counting each snowflake until the number was exactly 3 million, 471 thousand, 952. Then with the settling of the very next flake—*crack*. The branch suddenly snapped, tumbling the mouse and the snow to the ground. "Humph . . . Such was the weight of nothing," said the mouse.

So the next time you think your contributions, your acts of charity, your works for justice, your gifts of love, and your talents are nothing, or that they are small in comparison to those of others, remember that when one is added to another, and then to another and so forth, great things can happen from nothing. In the same way, what seems to be ordinary can be transformed into something extraordinary with just a little extra nothing.

So, too, [United Way] transforms a community that shares with each other's own nothingness, and one's ordinary gifts and talents are united to strengthen the whole. [United Way's] mission is to create great things once again out of nothingness, to transform the ordinary into the extraordinary.

71.
The Most Valuable Treasure

Anonymous

There is a city in Germany named Weinsberg. Overlooking the city, perched atop a high hill, stands an ancient fortress.

The townspeople of Weinsberg are proud to tell about an interesting legend concerning the fortress.

According to the legend, in the 15th century, in the days of chivalry and honor, enemy troops laid siege to the fortress and sealed all the townsfolk inside. The enemy commander sent word up to the fortress announcing that he would allow the women and children to leave and go free before he launched a devastating attack.

After some negotiations, the enemy commander also agreed, on his word of honor, to let each woman take with her the most valuable, personal treasure she possessed, provided she could carry it out herself.

You can imagine the enemy commander's consternation and surprise when the women began marching out of the fortress . . . each one carrying her husband on her back.

72.
Grandfather's Cure

Unknown

A while back there was an episode on *The Cosby Show* in which 16-year-old Theo talks with his best friend about this other guy who was paying too much attention to Theo's girlfriend. Theo's friend tells him about his brother who once had a similar problem and that he got the other guy to vanish by going to the voodoo doctor.

Theo is uncertain what to think—a voodoo doctor? However, after a while the two of them are standing outside the door to the apartment of the voodoo doctor. They hesitate. "Go ahead and knock," says Theo.

"No, you! She's your girl, not mine," his friend responds.

Theo knocks and a man in an obviously expensive suit opens the door. "What do you want?" he asks.

Theo tells his story and asks the man if he can help him

with this problem. The voodoo man says he can help. And Theo asks him, "How can you do that?"

The voodoo doctor explains: "I take a chicken foot, dip the claws into vinegar, and on a sheet of old parchment I write the boy's name backwards. I then burn the paper and sprinkle the ashes over the chicken foot and the boy disappears— guaranteed."

Theo asks, "How much will this cost?"

"$900!" the man tells him.

"Say what, $900? Where can I get that much money?" Theo struggles with his problem and finally decides to ask his father for a loan.

Dr. Huxtable listens to Theo's request and blurts out, "You want how much? $900 for a voodoo doctor's fee to make some guy disappear who's paying too much attention to your girl?" Dr. Huxtable relates a similar problem he had when he was about Theo's age and how his father came up with a cure that didn't cost anything. Theo asks his dad if he thought Grandfather's cure would work for him, too. Dr. Huxtable leads Theo into the kitchen and says, "Tell you what I'm going to do. Sit down, my son."

He has Theo open up his hands, palm up and smears peanut butter all over the hands. He goes into the pantry for a bag of navy beans and sprinkles beans on top of the peanut butter, and then pours cooking oil on top of both. Suddenly from behind Theo Dr. Huxtable shouts, "*Cover your eyes!*"

Thwack! . . . what a yucky mess.

Dr. Huxtable takes a towel and fashions it into a turban on Theo's head. He hands Theo a large cookie sheet and a wooden spoon and tells him to march around the kitchen table banging the cookie sheet while chanting, "I will pay more attention to my girlfriend. I will pay more attention to my girlfriend. I will pay more attention. . . ."

About the fourth time around the table, Theo got the message. He began paying more attention to his girlfriend and, you know what, the cure worked again! The other guy soon vanished.

Grandfather Huxtable's cure will work today if you need to pay more attention to someone or something.

73.
Don't Quit
(gender inclusive)

Clinton Howell

When things go wrong, as they sometimes will,
When the road you're trudging seems all up hill,
When the funds are low and the debts are high,
And you want to smile, but you have to sigh,
When care is pressing you down a bit,
Rest, if you must—but don't you quit.

Life is strange with its twists and turns,
As everyone of us sometimes learns,
And many a failure turns about
When he or she might have won had one stuck it out;
Don't give up, though the pace seems slow—
You might succeed with another blow.

Often the goal is nearer than
It seems to a faint and faltering woman or man,
Often the struggler has given up
When one might have captured the victor's cup.
And he or she learned too late, when the night slipped
    down,
How close one was to the golden crown.

Success is failure turned inside out—
The silver tint of the clouds of doubt—
And you never can tell how close you are,
It may be near when it seems afar;
So stick to the fight when you're hardest hit—
It's when things seem worst that you must not quit.

74.
Power To Fly

Anonymous

Ultimately we have the power to decide what we believe about ourselves. Don't allow people to impose limitations on what you can do or whom you can become. Take, for instance, the humble bumble bee.

Biologists have determined that, aerodynamically speaking, the bumble bee cannot fly. It has too large of a body mass to be supported by such puny wings. The bumble bee fortunately does not listen to such criticism.

Remember: People rise no higher than their expectation level. Expect little, receive little. Expect to fly and who knows where your next flower might be?

75.
Prayer for Tongue Control

Anonymous

O Lord, keep me from getting talkative. And particularly from the fatal habit that I must say something on every subject at every occasion.

Release me from craving to straighten out everybody's affairs.

Keep my mind free from the recital of endless details; give me wings to get to the point. Seal my lips when inclined to tell of my aches and pains.

They are increasing with the years and my love of rehearing them grows sweeter as the years go by.

Teach me the glorious lesson that occasionally it is possible that I may be mistaken.

Keep me reasonably sweet. I do not want to be a saint. Some of them are hard to live with, but a sour old woman or man is one of the crowning works of the devil.

Help me to extract all possible fun out of life. There are so
  many funny things around us, and I do not want to miss
  any of them.
Make me thoughtful but not moody, helpful but not bossy.
With my vast store of wisdom, it seems a pity not to use it
  all. But you, my Lord, know that I want a few friends
  left at the end.
Amen.

76.

Wantivation

Thomas Harris

Thomas Harris is quoted as saying there are three things
that give people the *wantivation* to change:

1. They must hurt sufficiently;
2. They must experience despair or boredom;
3. They must suddenly discover they can change.

77.

A Ripple of Hope

Robert F. Kennedy

When God made you, he threw away the mold. There
never has been or ever will be another person just like you.
The late Robert F. Kennedy addressed the young people of
South Africa in 1966 with the following passage. The same
passage was used by Ted Kennedy in his eulogy at his brother
Robert's funeral.

"Some believe there is nothing one man or one woman
can do against the enormous array of the world's ills. Yet many

of the world's great movements of thought and action have flowed from the work of a single person. . . .

"These people moved the world, and so can we all. Few will have the greatness to bend history itself, but each person can work to change a small portion of events, and in the total of all those acts will be written the history of this generation.

"It is from numberless diverse acts of courage and belief that human history is shaped. Each time a person stands up for an ideal, or acts to improve the lot of others, or strikes out against injustice, he or she sends forth a tiny ripple of hope. And crossing each other from a million different centers of energy and daring, those ripples build a current that can sweep down the mightiest walls of oppression and resistance."

78.
The King's Great Gift

Anonymous

There once was a wise and beloved king who cared greatly for his people and wanted only what was the best for them. The people knew the king took a personal interest in their affairs and tried to understand how his decisions affected their lives. Periodically, he would disguise himself and wander through the streets, trying to see life from their perspective.

One day he disguised himself as a poor villager and went to visit the public baths. Many people were there enjoying the fellowship and relaxation. The water for the baths was heated by a furnace in the cellar, where one man was responsible for maintaining the comfort level of the water. The king made his way to the basement to visit with the man who tirelessly tended the fire.

The two men shared a meal together, and the king befriended this lonely man. Day after day, week in and week out, the king went to visit the firetender. The man in the cellar soon became close to his strange visitor because he came down to the basement where he was. No one else ever had showed that much caring or concern.

One day the king revealed his true identity to his friend. It was a risky move, for he feared that the man might ask him for special favors or a gift. Instead, the king's new friend looked into his eyes and said, "You left your comfortable palace to sit with me in this hot and dingy cellar. You ate my meager food and genuinely showed you cared about what happens to me. On other people you might bestow rich gifts, but to me you have given the greatest gift of all. You gave me the gift of yourself."

79.
Great Value in Disaster

Anonymous

Thomas Edison's laboratory was virtually destroyed by fire in December, 1914. Although the damage exceeded two million dollars, the buildings were only insured for $238,000 because they were made of concrete and thought to be fireproof. Much of Edison's life's work went up in spectacular flames that December night.

At the height of the fire, Edison's 24-year-old son, Charles, frantically searched for his father among the smoke and debris. He finally found him, calmly watching the scene, his face glowing in the reflection, his white hair blowing in the wind.

"My heart ached for him," said Charles. "He was 67 — no longer a young man — and everything was going up in flames. When he saw me, he shouted, 'Charles, where's your mother?' When I told him I didn't know, he said, 'Find her. Bring her here. She will never see anything like this as long as she lives.' "

The next morning, Edison looked at the ruins and declared, "There is great value in disaster. All our mistakes are burned up. Thank God, we can start anew."

Three weeks after the fire, Edison managed to deliver the first phonograph.

80.
Making Progress

Anonymous

When Pablo Casals reached ninety-five years of age, a reporter asked him a question. "Mr. Casals," inquired the reporter, "you are ninety-five now and acclaimed as the greatest cellist that ever lived. Why do you still practice six hours a day?"

Mr. Casals put down his bow and replied, "Because I think I'm making progress."

Not a bad goal, to make a little progress every day of your life.

81.
Gave Up Too Soon!

Anonymous

Thayer Lindsley's chance to build one of the great mining fortunes in Canada came because Thomas Edison simply gave up too soon. In 1901, the famous inventor was searching for a reliable supply of nickel that he needed for building storage batteries. Edison staked out claims around the small township of Falconbridge, near Sudbury, Ontario. When the exploratory drilling hit quicksand, Edison turned to other sources, and the mining claims lay idle until the 1920s, when Lindsley came along.

As founder of a company aptly named Ventures, Lindsley

was so sure of finding ore that he bought the old Edison claims for a seemingly enormous sum of $2.5 million. It turned out to be a paltry investment compared to what became Falconbridge, one of the largest mining concerns in the world.

82.
Reconcile Petty Squabbles

Anonymous

A silly argument left two sisters bitter after the death of their mother. For years, they barely spoke, and rarely saw one another. If the truth were known, they could hardly remember what the "squabble" was about. An aunt thought it was over a piece of cheap costume jewelry they both wanted because it "looked so much like mother."

One night the seventeen-year-old son of the younger sister was seriously injured in a car wreck. When word reached the boy's estranged aunt, her heart was broken. Visions of her own son raced through her mind as she began to weep. She also pictured the tormented face of her younger sister. As she thought about her, she saw her as a little girl playing with her dolls; a teenager getting ready for her first date; a beautiful bride; a wife; a mother. The "squabble" seemed so petty now.

The older sister jumped into her car and raced across town to the hospital where her sister's family was waiting . . . praying for the boy. When she entered the hospital waiting room and saw her sister for the first time in years, she ran to her, hugged her, and said, "I'm sorry."

How sad that she didn't say it sooner. How wonderful that she did and how wonderful that she became reconciled with her sister before any more precious time passed! What about you? Are there any petty squabbles in your life that need to be reconciled?

83.
Who Will Play Second Fiddle?

Anonymous

The late great conductor Leonard Bernstein once was asked which instrument in the orchestra was the most difficult to play.

The maestro gave a surprising answer. "Second fiddle," he said promptly. "I can get plenty of first violinists. But to find someone who can play second fiddle with enthusiasm— that's a problem. Yet, if there is no one to play second fiddle, there is no harmony."

84.
The Day the Bull Stood in the Road
(adapted)

Ruth Dreyer

One day I was standing on a road. This road is known by many names: Life, Growth, Achievement, Faith, Happiness . . . I was just standing there, looking at something on the road up ahead. The thing I saw was a huge, mean-looking bull. And this bull was blocking my path. I knew that to keep moving ahead I was going to have to get past that bull. It scared me just to think about it. For a long, long time I stood still, looking at the bull, hoping and praying it would somehow move from my path so I could continue along the road. However, nothing changed, except that I heard a distant voice whisper, "Do whatever it is you have to do in order to continue along the journey."

That was the day I decided to take a deep breath, gather all the strength I could muster, and take the bull by the horns. I knew that in so doing I would have to accept whatever consequences followed—good, bad, or indifferent. Having decided to be completely responsible for whatever happened to me, I set aside my doubts and fears and marched right up to that bull, grabbed those horns, and said, "All right, bull! You've got to get out of my way or fight with me—which will it be?"

Well, you'll never believe what happened next! That crazy bull sat down right on the road, sighed and spoke to me. "What took you so long getting here?" he asked. "I've been standing here waiting to offer you a ride. Hop up on my back and show me where it is you want to go."

What was thought to be an insurmountable problem turned out to be a great blessing instead. All that I needed was the courage to discover the blessing.

85.
What's the Problem?

Anonymous

There was a professor who walked into the classroom, and wrote three numbers on the blackboard: *2 4 8*. He turned to the class and asked, "So, what's the solution?"

Some students said, "Add them up for 14." The professor shook his head.

Others said, "It's a progression, and 16 is the next number." The professor shook his head.

A group in the back said, "64." Again the professor shook his head.

"No," said the professor. "You all hurried into finding a solution, but you failed to ask, 'What is the problem?' Unless you ask that key question, you cannot know what the problem is, nor can you possibly find the solution."

He's right. It's almost so simple we forget about it. Most of us are quick to give answers without first making certain that we know what is the real problem.

86.
Come Unto Me

Anonymous

A well-known sculptor had a burning ambition to create the greatest statue of Jesus Christ ever made. He began in his oceanside studio by shaping a clay model of a triumphant, regal figure. The head was thrown back and the arms were upraised in a gesture of great majesty. It was his conception of how Christ would look: strong and dominant.

"This will be my masterpiece," he said, on the day the clay model was completed.

During the night, however, a heavy fog rolled into the area and sea spray seeped through a partially opened window. The moisture affected the shape of the clay so that when the artist returned to the studio in the morning, he was shocked at what he found.

Droplets of moisture had formed on the model creating an illusion of bleeding. The head had drooped. The facial expression had been transformed from one of severity to one of compassion. And the arms had dropped into a posture of welcome. It had become a wounded Christ-figure.

The artist stared at the figure, agonizing over the time wasted and the need to begin all over again. Then, inspiration came over him to change his mood. He began to see that this image of Christ was, by far, the truer one. So he carved these words in the base of the newly shaped figure: *Come Unto Me.*

87.
How To Worship

Anonymous

In the back of a frequently visited church in a bustling part of the city there was a sign that read:

How to Worship:

Be silent.
Be thoughtful.
Be reverent, for this is the House of the Lord.
Before the service, speak to God.
During the service, let God speak to you.
After the service, speak to one another.

88.
Takes Toil To Bloom

Dorman Winger

One hot summer afternoon a woman was working strenuously, weeding her flower beds and pruning the plants. The flowers were especially magnificent.

A passerby asked, "I really like those flowers—do you?"

As she wiped perspiration from her face with a dirty hand, the woman's weary response was, "Only when they bloom."

The passerby thought how many folks have a similar attitude toward church, family, work, or life in general—"I only like it when it is in full bloom and beautiful."

The passerby thought of those necessary times of hard work—mulching, weeding, cultivating, pruning and transplanting—as well as seasonal dormancy, which are all necessary to bring about the blooms which precede the bearing of seeds and fruit.

89.
Can't Please Everybody

Anonymous

The director of religious education was showing off the First Communion class for the benefit of the pastor. She tried to gauge her questions to their intelligence levels so that each child would make a good showing.

"Johnny," she said to one of the boys, "is there anything God cannot do?"

"Yes, sister," Johnny replied confidently.

"Think again, Johnny," she repeated. "Is there anything God cannot do?"

"Yes, sister, there is," came the same reply with more emphasis than before.

"O.K., Johnny, what is it?" asked the sister in exasperation. Johnny replied triumphantly, "God can't please everybody!"

90.
Do You Know Me?

Anonymous

I have no respect for justice. I maim without killing. I break hearts and ruin lives. I am cunning and malicious and gather strength with age.

The more I am quoted, the more I am believed. I flourish at every level of society.

My victims are helpless. They cannot protect themselves against me, for I have no face and no name. To track me down is impossible. The harder you try, the more elusive I become.

I am nobody's friend. Once I tarnish a reputation, it is never quite the same.

I topple governments and wreck marriages. I ruin careers, and cause sleepless nights, heartaches, and grief. I make innocent people cry into their pillow. I make headlines and heartaches.

I am called gossip!

The next time you want to tell a story about someone . . . think. Is it true? Is it necessary? Is it kind? If not, please don't say it!

91.
The Greatest Ability

Anonymous

There are great abilities that people acquire, cultivate and demonstrate. In the service of God, however, there is one ability that is the greatest ability of all. What is it? Is it sociability? Compatibility? Accountability? Adaptability? Reliability?

The greatest ability is *availability*. If we are not available to God, no matter what other kinds of ability we have, our ability is no good. Ability without availability is a liability.

Availability means that there is a sense of preparedness and readiness. There are people in life who are prepared, but they simply are not available.

Sometimes people assume God cannot use them because they do not have great abilities, special talents or gifted aptitudes. They feel they are just ordinary and do not have anything special for God's use. But God never asks about our ability, only about our availability.

92.
A Reflection of Your Image

Anonymous

I am your (church, community, family . . .). Make of me what you will; I shall reflect you as clearly as a mirror. If outwardly my appearance is pleasing and inviting, it is because you have made me so. If within my spiritual atmosphere is kindly, yet earnest; reverent, yet friendly; worshipful, yet sympathetic; divine, yet humanly expressed, it is but the manifestation of the spirit of those who constitute my membership.

But if you should, by chance, find me a bit cold or dull, I beg of you not to condemn me, for I imitate the kind of life I receive from you. Of this you may always be assured; I will respond instantly to your every wish practically expressed, for I reflect the image of your own soul. Make of me what you will.

93.
The Wedding Ring

Anonymous

Some years ago divers located a 400-year-old sunken ship off the coast of Ireland. Among the treasures they found on the ship was a man's wedding ring. When it was cleaned up, the divers noticed that the ring had an inscription on it. Etched on the wide band were two hands holding a heart. Under the etching were these words: "I have nothing more to give you."

Of all the treasures found on that sunken ship, none moved the divers more than that ring and its beautiful inscription.

94.
What Do You See?

Anonymous

A wise old archer was training two young warriors. Across the meadow was a small target hanging from a tree.

The first warrior took an arrow from his quiver, readied it in his bow, and took aim. The old archer asked him to describe everything he saw. "I see the sky, the clouds, the trees, and leaves, the branches and the target," he answered.

"Put your bow down," the old archer said. "You are not ready."

The second warrior stepped up and readied his bow with an arrow. The old man ordered him, "Describe everything you see."

"There is only the target," said the second warrior.

"Then, shoot!" was the command. The arrow flew straight and hit the target. "Very good," said the old archer. "When you see only the target, your aim will be true, and your arrows will fly according to your wish."

To focus our thinking does not come easily, but it is a skill that can be developed, a skill that is as valuable in life as in archery.

95.
High Wind, Big Thunder, No Rain!

Anonymous

A Native American Indian attended a Sunday morning worship service. The sermon contained very little in the way of spiritual food and had been delivered in rather loud tones. The Native American was a faithful Christian, but was not impressed with the preaching.

On the way out of church the minister asked him if he liked the sermon. His reply was, "High wind, big thunder, no rain!"

96.
Prayer and Studies

Anonymous

A student, rather lazily inclined, noticed that a classmate always recited her Spanish lessons well. One day he asked her, "How is it that you always recite your lessons so perfectly?"

"Before I study," she told him, "I always pray that I may remember my lessons and repeat them well."

"Do you?" said the boy somewhat surprised. "So that's her secret method," he thought. "Well, then, I'll pray too." That night he prayed up a storm, recalling as many prayers as he could remember. However, the next day he could not even repeat one phrase of the lesson. Quite perplexed he looked for his friend, and, finding her, confronted her for being deceitful.

"I prayed," he told her, "but I could not repeat a single phrase from yesterday's homework."

"Perhaps," she told him, "you took no pains to learn the lesson!"

"Of course not," said the boy. "I didn't study at all. I had no reason to study. You told me to pray that I might remember the lesson."

"There's your problem," she said, "I told you I prayed *before*, not instead of, studying."

97.
A Year of Time (adapted)

Steven B. Cloud

Though even thinking on the subject of time may prove discomforting, it is not a bad idea, especially at the beginning of a new year.

As we look back into [year?] we look at a block of time. We see 12 months, 52 weeks, 365 days, 8,760 hours, 525,600 minutes, 31,536,000 seconds. All is a gift from God. We have done nothing to deserve it, earn it, or purchase it. Like the air we breathe, time comes to us as a part of life.

But the gift of time is not ours alone. It is given equally to each person. Rich and poor, educated and ignorant, strong and weak—every man, woman, and child has the exact same 24 hours, 1,440 minutes and 86,400 seconds every day.

Another important thing about time is that you cannot stop it. There is no way to slow it down, turn it off, or adjust it. Time marches on. In addition, you cannot bring back time. Once it is gone, it is gone. Yesterday is lost forever.

If yesterday is lost, tomorrow is uncertain. We may look

ahead at a full year's block of time, but we really have no guarantee that we will experience any part of it.

Time is obviously one of our most precious possessions. We can waste it, worry over it, spend it on ourselves. Or, as good stewards, we can invest it in building up the kingdom of God.

The new year is full of time. As the seconds tick away, will you be tossing time out the window, or will you make every minute count?

98.
Make It Happen

Anonymous

The great Thomas Alva Edison discouraged his friend, Henry Ford, from pursuing his fledgling idea of a motorcar. Convinced of the worthlessness of the project, Edison invited Ford to come and work for him. Thankfully, Ford remained committed to his idea and tirelessly pursued his dream. Although his first attempt resulted in a vehicle without a reverse gear, Ford knew he could make it happen. And, eventually, he did.

"Forget it," the experts advised Madame Marie Curie. They agreed that radium could not exist. However, Marie Curie insisted, "I know radium is a real element. I can make it happen." And that she did.

Let's not forget the Wright Brothers either. Journalists, friends, specialists, and even their father laughed at the folly of their idea for an airplane. "What a silly and insane way to waste money," Orville and Wilbur were told. Others jeered, "Leave flying to the birds."

"Sorry," the brothers replied. "We have a dream, and we can make it happen." As a result, a place named Kitty Hawk, North Carolina, became the setting for the launching of their "ridiculous" idea.

Finally, consider the plight of Benjamin Franklin the next time you marvel at the modern conveniences we take for granted—television, computers, air conditioning, stereos, blenders, etc., all of which work by simply plugging them into a wall outlet. He was admonished to stop his foolish experiments with lightning. What an absurd waste of time! Why, nothing could outdo the oil lamp. Thank goodness, Franklin knew he could make electricity happen.

Do you have an idea, a dream, a burning desire? You, too, can make it happen.

99.
Don't Lose Your Presence of Mind

Anonymous

Dear Sir:

I'm writing in response to your request for additional information. In block #3 of the accident reporting form, I put "poor planning" as the cause of my accident. You said that I should explain more fully, and I trust the following details will be sufficient.

I'm a bricklayer by trade, and on the day of the accident, I was working alone on the roof of a new six-story building. When I completed my work, I discovered that I had about a strap-and-a-half of bricks left over. Rather than carrying the bricks down by hand, I decided to lower them in a barrel by using a pulley, which fortunately was attached to the building at the sixth floor. Securing the rope at the ground level, I went up to the roof, swung the barrel out, and loaded the bricks into it. Then I hurried back to the ground and untied the rope, holding it tightly to ensure a slow descent of the 500+ pounds of bricks. You will note in block #11 of the accident reporting form that I weigh 135 pounds.

Due to my surprise at being jerked off my feet so suddenly, I lost my presence of mind, and forgot to let go of the rope. Needless to say, I proceeded at a rather rapid rate up the side of the building. In the vicinity of the third floor, I met the barrel coming down. This explains the fractured skull and broken collarbone. Slowed only ever so slightly, I continued my rapid ascent, not stopping until the fingers of my right hand were two knuckles deep into the pulley.

Fortunately, by this time I had regained my presence of mind, and was still able to hold tightly to the rope in spite of the intense pain. At approximately the same time, however, the barrel of bricks hit the ground and the bottom fell out of the barrel. Now devoid of the bricks, the barrel weighed only fifty pounds. I refer you again to my weight in box #11. As you might imagine, I began a rapid descent down the side of the building. In the vicinity of the third floor, I again met the barrel, now going up. This accounts for the two fractured ankles and the lacerations on my legs and lower body. This time the encounter with the barrel slowed me enough to lessen my injuries when I landed on the pile of bricks, and only three vertebrae were cracked.

I am sorry to report, however, that as I lay there on the bricks in pain, unable to stand and watching the empty barrel six stories above me, I again lost my presence of mind. I let go of the rope . . . and . . .

100.
Oil of Kindness

Anonymous

There was an old man who carried a little can of oil with him everywhere he went, and if he passed through a door that squeaked, he put a little oil on the hinges. If a gate was hard to open, he oiled the latch. So he passed through life lubricating all the creaking places, making it easier for those who came after him.

People called him eccentric, strange, cranky, odd, and

even harsher names. But the old man went steadily on, refilling his can of oil when it became empty and oiling the squeaking places he found. He did not wait until he found a creaky door or a rusty hinge, and then go home to get his oil can; he carried it with him at all times.

There are many lives that creak and squeak and grate harshly day by day. They need lubricating with the oil of kindness, gentleness, or thoughtfulness. That can of oil is one of the predominant characteristics of a Christian life. Such a can of oil we are to carry around with us at all times.

Source Acknowledgments

This book is the fruition of years of reading, listening and transcribing stories from many and varied sources. I thank the authors and publishers who have given their generous cooperation and permission to include these stories in this collection. Further reproduction without permission is prohibited.

Every effort has been made to acknowledge the proper source for each story; regrettably, I am unable to give proper credit to every story. When the proper source becomes known, proper credit will be given in future editions of this book.

DO WHAT NEEDS TO BE DONE
    Anonymous
    Source Unknown

CONSIDER THE WALNUT
    Anonymous
    Source Unknown

THE GOSPEL ACCORDING TO YOU
    Anonymous
    Source Unknown

GIVING OR KEEPING
    Anonymous
    Source Unknown

CHUCK YEAGER—THE RIGHT STUFF
Chuck Yeager
Yeager

ALPHABET PRAYER
Anonymous
Source Unknown

CONQUER WEAKNESSES
Anonymous
Source Unknown

WE'VE LOST SIGHT OF CHRISTMAS
Brian Cavanaugh, T.O.R.
Christmas Season homily inspiration
Adapted from *Sunday Sermon Masterpiece Illustrations*

ART IS SO EASY
Anonymous
Source Unknown

THE PRICELESS INGREDIENT
Anonymous
1921 advertisement
E.R. Squibb & Sons

A MOTHER'S PARAPHRASE OF
1 CORINTHIANS 13
Mrs. Mervin Seashore
Source Unknown

WITH ENTHUSIASM
Anonymous
Source Unknown

THE TIGER CUB THAT ROARED
Anonymous
Source Unknown

THE BRILLIANT ILLITERATE
Anonymous
Source Unknown

TOWN WITH FOUR NEIGHBORHOODS
(ADAPTED)
Jim Savage
"Top Performance," Vol. 2, #6

ART OF CONVERSATION
Anonymous
Source Unknown

PLANTING BIG POTATOES
Anonymous
Pulpit Helps, Vol. 14, #2

ATTITUDE DETERMINES RESPONSE
Anonymous
Source Unknown

A LEADER KNOWS
Chinese Proverb
Source Unknown

UNNOTICED VALUE
Anonymous
Source Unknown

WHERE ARE YOUR ABILITIES?
Anonymous
Source Unknown

LETTER ON HUMILITY
C. S. Lewis
The Screwtape Letters, Letter XIV
NY: Bantam Books, 1982
Used with permission

COMPANIONS—"WITH BREAD" (ADAPTED)
Rev. Robert McAfee Brown
Life magazine

FULFILLED DREAMS, BURNING DESIRE
Anonymous
Source Unknown

VISION OF THE SNAIL
Anonymous
Source Unknown

TELLER OF NEW TRUTHS
Merle Crowell
Source Unknown

TRAGEDY OR BLESSING?
Anonymous
Source Unknown

ART OF LEADERSHIP
Anonymous
Source Unknown

THE MIRACLE BRIDGE
Anonymous
Source Unknown

"METAMORPHOSIS"
Anonymous
Source Unknown

THE ERRANT KNIGHT OF ASSISI
Brian Cavanaugh, T.O.R.
Adapted from an American folktale

GARDEN OF THE MIND
James Allen
As a Man Thinketh
NY: G.P. Putnam's Sons

KINDNESS WINS MORE FANS
Anonymous
Source Unknown

"POST-IT NOTES" STORY
Anonymous
Source Unknown

WRANGLERS VS. STRANGLERS
Ted Engstrom
Source Unknown

ST. FRANCIS DE SALES VISITS ROME
Anonymous
Source Unknown

TAME THE WILDNESS
Anonymous
Source Unknown

SURVIVAL FROM A GULAG
Anonymous
Source Unknown

STILL ROPE, STILL HOPE
Anonymous
Source Unknown

A DIFFERENT VISION
Joseph Girzone
Joshua
Macmillan, 1987

NEVER LOSE SIGHT OF GOALS
Anonymous
Source Unknown

GOOD NEWS REPORT
Anonymous
Source Unknown

SHORTCUTS IN LIFE
Zig Ziglar
See You at the Top
Gretna, LA: Pelican Publishing, 1977

EARTHY MYSTICISM
John Donne
Source Unknown

A SHORT-SIGHTED BISHOP
Anonymous
Source Unknown

THE BEATITUDES: THE LESSON
Anonymous
Source Unknown

COMPASSION IS IN THE EYES
Anonymous
Source Unknown

GOD WHO ENABLES
Faye Sweeney
Source Unknown

THE CLUMP OF GRASS
Brian Cavanaugh, T.O.R.
Source Unknown

A TON OF BRICKS
Brian Cavanaugh, T.O.R.
Personal Account

OBSTACLE OR OPPORTUNITY
Anonymous
Source Unknown

IT'S IN YOUR HANDS
Anonymous
Source Unknown

THE TRAVELER AND THE SHEPHERD
Anonymous
Source Unknown

ONLY CHEATING YOURSELF
Anonymous
Source Unknown

PUBLIC SPEAKING QUALIFICATIONS
Anonymous
Source Unknown

LETTER TO DIOGENTUS
Anonymous, 2nd century A.D.
Source Unknown

LIVES OUT OF BALANCE
Anonymous
Source Unknown

THE ORIGINS OF THE CHRISTMAS CRIB
from *The Life of St. Francis (Legenda Maior)*
by St. Bonaventure, in
Bonaventure (The Classics of Western Spirituality),
pp. 278–279
Mahwah, NJ: Paulist Press, 1978
Used with permission

A SIMPLE GESTURE
Anonymous
Source Unknown

LOST ISLAND LEGEND
Brian Cavanaugh, T.O.R.
Sunday Homily

HEAVEN OR HELL?
Anonymous
Source Unknown

TOWARD SELF-DESTRUCTION
Anonymous
Source Unknown

BE A LAMPLIGHTER
Brian Cavanaugh, T.O.R.
Sunday Homily

MAKE A DIFFERENCE
Anonymous
Source Unknown

NIGHT AND DAY
Anonymous
Source Unknown

IMPORTANCE OF THE OBVIOUS
Anonymous
Source Unknown

MEANING OF CHRISTMAS
Anonymous
Source Unknown

SECRET OF SUCCESS (ADAPTED)
Clarence DeLoach, Jr.
Source Unknown

RATING CODE FOR SERMONS
Anonymous
Source Unknown

THE WEIGHT OF A SNOWFLAKE (ADAPTED)
Anonymous
Source Unknown

THE MOST VALUABLE TREASURE
Anonymous
Source Unknown

GRANDFATHER'S CURE
Unknown
Paraphrased from
The Cosby Show

DON'T QUIT
Clinton Howell
Source Unknown

POWER TO FLY
Anonymous
Source Unknown

PRAYER FOR TONGUE CONTROL
Anonymous
Source Unknown

WANTIVATION
Thomas Harris
Source Unknown

A RIPPLE OF HOPE
Robert F. Kennedy
Source Unknown

THE KING'S GREAT GIFT
Anonymous
Source Unknown

GREAT VALUE IN DISASTER
Anonymous
Source Unknown

MAKING PROGRESS
Anonymous
Source Unknown

GAVE UP TOO SOON!
Anonymous
Source Unknown

RECONCILE PETTY SQUABBLES
Anonymous
"Top Performance," Vol. 3, #6

WHO WILL PLAY SECOND FIDDLE?
Anonymous
Source Unknown

THE WEDDING RING
Anonymous
Source Unknown

WHAT DO YOU SEE?
Anonymous
Source Unknown

HIGH WIND, BIG THUNDER, NO RAIN!
Anonymous
Source Unknown

PRAYER AND STUDIES
Anonymous
Source Unknown

A YEAR OF TIME (ADAPTED)
Steven B. Cloud
Pulpit Helps, Vol. 14, #2

MAKE IT HAPPEN
Anonymous
Source Unknown

DON'T LOSE YOUR PRESENCE OF MIND
Anonymous
Source Unknown

OIL OF KINDNESS
Anonymous
Source Unknown

Storytelling Reading List

Abrahams, Roger D., ed. *African Folktales: Traditional Stories of the Black World.* NY: Pantheon Books–Random House, 1983.

Aesop's Fables. London: Bracken Books, 1986.

Afasas'ev, Aleksandr, ed. *Russian Fairy Tales.* NY: Pantheon Books–Random House, 1973.

Allen, James. *As a Man Thinketh.* NY: G.P. Putnam's Sons.

Applebaum, Rabbi Morton and Rabbi Samuel M. Silver, eds. *Speak to the Children of Israel.* KTAV Publishing House, Inc., 1976.

Arcodia, Charles. *Stories for Sharing.* Newtown, Australia: E.J. Dwyer, Ltd., 1991.

Aurelio, John. *Story Sunday.* NY: Paulist Press, 1978.

———. *Fables for God's People.* NY: Crossroad, 1988.

Ausubel, Nathan, ed. *A Treasury of Jewish Folklore.* NY: Crown Publishers, 1948.

Barker, Esther T. *The Unused Cradle.* Nashville: The Upper Room, 1968.

Bausch, William. *Storytelling: Imagination and Faith.* Mystic, CT: Twenty-Third Publications, 1984.

Bell, Martin. *The Way of the Wolf: Stories, Poems, Songs and Thoughts on the Parables of Jesus.* NY: Ballantine Books/Epiphany Edition, 1983.

Benjamin, Don-Paul, Ron Miner. *Come Sit With Me Again: Sermons for Children.* NY: The Pilgrim Press, 1987.

Bettelheim, Bruno. *The Uses of Enchantment.* NY: Vintage Books, 1977.

Bodo, OFM, Murray. *Tales of St. Francis: Ancient Stories for Contemporary Living.* NY: Doubleday, 1988.

Book of Christmas, A: Readings for Reflection during Advent and Christmas. Nashville: The Upper Room, 1988.

Boyer, Mark. *Following the Star: Daily Reflections for Advent and Christmas*. Liguori, MO: Liguori Publications, 1989.

Briggs, Katharine. *An Encyclopedia of Fairies*. NY: Pantheon Books–Random House, 1976.

Brunvand, Jan Harold. *Curses! Broiled Again!* NY: W.W. Norton & Co., 1989.

Buber, Martin. *Tales of the Hasidim: Early Masters*. NY: Schocken Books, 1975.

———. *Tales of the Hasidim: Later Masters*. NY: Schocken Books, 1948.

Bushnaq, Inea, ed. *Arab Folktales*. NY: Pantheon Books–Random House, 1986.

Byrd, Charles W. *The Fall of the Sparrow*. Lima, OH: C.S.S. Publishing Company, Inc., 1990.

Calvino, Italo, ed. *Italian Folktales*. NY: Pantheon Books–Random House, 1980.

Carroll, James. *Wonder and Worship*. NY: Newman Press, 1970.

Cassady, Marsh. *Storytelling: Step by Step*. San Jose, CA: Resource Publications, 1990.

Castagnola, S.J., Larry. *More Parables for Little People*. San Jose, CA: Resource Publications, Inc, 1987.

Cattan, Henry. *The Garden of Joys: An Anthology of Oriental Anecdotes, Fables and Proverbs*. London: Namara Publications, Ltd, 1979.

Cavanaugh, Brian, T.O.R. *The Sower's Seeds: One Hundred Inspiring Stories for Preaching, Teaching and Public Speaking*. Mahwah, NJ: Paulist Press, 1990.

———. *More Sower's Seeds: Second Planting*. Mahwah, NJ: Paulist Press, 1992.

Chalk, Gary. *Tales of Ancient China*. London: Frederick Muller, 1984.

Chappell, Stephen, O.S.B. *Dragons & Demons, Angels & Eagles: Morality Tales for Teens*. St. Louis: Liguori Publications, 1990.

Charlton, James and Barbara Gilson, eds. *A Christmas Trea-*

sury of *Yuletide Stories & Poems*. NY: Galahad Books–LDAP, 1992.

Clark, Susan. *Celebrating Earth Holy Days*. Intro. Thomas Berry. NY: Crossroad, 1992.

Colainni, James F., Sr., ed. *Sunday Sermons Treasury of Illustrations*. Pleasantville, NJ: Voicings Publications, 1982.

Colainni, James F., Jr., ed. *Contemportary Sermon Illustrations*. Ventor, NJ: Italicus, Inc., 1991.

Colum, Padraic, ed. *A Treasury of Irish Folklore*. 2nd ed. NY: Crown Publishers, Inc., 1967.

Complete Grimm's Fairy Tales, The. NY: Pantheon Books, 1972.

Cornils, Stanley, ed. *34 Two-Minute Talks for Youth and Adults*. Cincinnati, OH: Standard Publications, 1985.

Curtin, Jeremiah, ed. *Myths and Folk Tales of Ireland*. NY: Dover, 1975.

Dasent, George Webbe, ed. *East o' the Sun & West o' the Moon*. NY: Dover, 1970.

De La Fontaine, Jean, ed. *Selected Fables*. NY: Dover, 1968.

de Mello, Anthony, SJ. *The Song of the Bird*. India: Gujarat Sahitya Prakash, 1982.

————. *One Minute Wisdom*. NY: Doubleday & Co, 1986.

————. *Taking Flight*. NY: Doubleday, 1988.

————. *The Heart of the Enlightened*. NY: Doubleday, 1989.

————. *One Minute Nonsense*. Chicago: Loyola University Press, 1992.

————. *More One Minute Nonsense*. Chicago: Loyola University Press, 1993.

Doleski, Teddi. *The Hurt*. Mahwah, NJ: Paulist Press, 1983.

————. *Silvester and the Oogaloo Boogaloo*. Mahwah, NJ: Paulist Press, 1990.

Erdoes, Richard and Alfonso Ortiz, eds. *American Indian Myths and Legends*. NY: Pantheon Books–Random House, 1984.

Evans, Ivor, ed. *Brewer's Dictionary of Phrase & Fable*. 14th ed. NY: Harper & Row, 1989.

103

Fahy, Mary. *The Tree That Survived the Winter*. Mahwah, NJ: Paulist Press, 1989.

Field, Claud, trans. *Jewish Legends of the Middle Ages*. London: Shapiro Vallentine & Co.

Frankel, Ellen. *The Classic Tales: 4,000 years of Jewish Lore*. Northvale, NJ: Jason Aronson, 1989.

Gates, Philip, ed. *Christmas in Song and Story*. NY: Cockcroft & Co., 1876.

Giono, Jean. *The Man Who Planted Trees*. Vermont: Chelsea Green Publishing Co., 1985.

Girzone, Joseph. *Joshua: A Parable for Today*. NY: Macmillan, 1983.

———. *Joshua and the Children*. NY: Macmillan, 1989.

Glassie, Henry, ed. *Irish Folk Tales*. NY: Pantheon Books– Random House, 1985.

Graves, Alfred. *The Irish Fairy Book*. NY: Greenwich House, 1983.

Hasler, Richard A. *God's Game Plan: Sports Anecdotes for Preachers*. Lima, OH: C.S.S. Publishing Company, Inc., 1990.

Haugaard, Erik Christian, trans. *Hans Christian Anderson: The Complete Fairy Tales and Stories*. NY: Anchor– Doubleday, 1974.

Haviland, Virginia, ed. *North American Legends*. NY: Philomel Books, 1979.

Hays, Edward. *Twelve and One-Half Keys*. Easton, KS: Forest of Peace Books, 1981.

———. *The Ethiopian Tattoo Shop*. Easton, KS: Forest of Peace Books, 1983.

———. *A Pilgrim's Almanac: Reflections for Each Day of the Year*. Easton, KS: Forest of Peace Books, Inc., 1989.

———. *The Christmas Eve Storyteller*. Easton, KS: Forest of Peace Books, 1992.

Henderschedt, James L. *The Magic Stone*. San Jose, CA: Resource Publications, Inc. (160 E. Virginia Street, S-290), 1988.

————. *The Topsy-Turvy Kingdom.* San Jose, CA: Resource Publications, Inc. (160 E. Virginia Street, S-290), 1990.

————. *The Light in the Lantern.* San Jose, CA: Resource Publications, Inc. (160 E. Virginia Street, S-290), 1991.

Holdcraft, Paul E., ed. *Snappy Stories for Sermons and Speeches.* Nashville: Abingdon Press, 1987.

Hunt, Angela Elwell. *The Tale of Three Trees: A Traditional Folktale.* Batavia, IL: Lion Publishing Corp., 1989 (1705 Hubbard Ave., Batavia, IL 60510).

Jeffers, Susan, ill. *Brother Eagle, Sister Sky: A Message from Chief Seattle.* NY: Penguin–Dial Books, 1991.

Johnson, Barry L. *The Visit of the Tomten.* Nashville: The Upper Room, 1981.

Johnson, Miriam. *Inside Twenty-Five Classic Children's Stories.* New York: Paulist Press, 1986.

Juknialis, Joseph. *Winter Dreams and other such friendly dragons.* San Jose, CA: Resource Publications, Inc, 1979.

Killinger, John. *Parables for Christmas.* Nashville: Abingdon Press, 1985.

————. *Christmas Spoken Here.* Nashville: Broadman Press, 1989.

Kronberg, Ruthilde and McKissack, Patricia C. *A Piece of the Wind and Other Stories to Tell.* NY: Harper & Row, 1990.

Lang, Andrew, ed. *The Brown Fairy Book.* NY: Dover, 1965.

Levin, Meyer. *Classic Hasidic Tales.* NY: Dorset Press, 1985.

Levine, David, ed. *The Fables of Aesop.* NY: Dorset Press, 1989.

Lewis, Naomi, ed. *Cry Wolf and Other Aesop Fables.* NY: Oxford University Press, 1988.

Lieberman, Leo and Beringause, Arthur. *Classics of Jewish Literature.* Secaucus, NJ: Book Sales, Inc., 1988.

Link, Mark, SJ. *Challenge.* Valencia, CA: Tabor Publications, 1988.

————. *Decision.* Valencia, CA: Tabor Publications, 1988.

————. *Journey.* Valencia, CA: Tabor Publications, 1988.

Livo, Norma J. and Sandra A. Rietz. *Storytelling: Process & Practice.* Littleton, CO: Libraries Unlimited, Inc., 1986.

————. *Storytelling Folklore Sourcebook*. Littleton, CO: Libraries Unlimited, Inc., 1991.

Lobel, Arnold. *Fables*. NY: HarperCollins, 1980.

Loder, Ted. *Tracks in the Snow: Tales Spun from the Manger*. San Diego, CA: LuraMedia, 1985.

Lufburrow, Bill. *Illustrations Without Sermons*. Nashville: Abingdon Press, 1985.

Magic Ox and other Tales of the Effendi, The. Beijing: Foreign Languages Press, 1986.

Marbach, Ethel. *The White Rabbit: A Franciscan Christmas Story*. Cincinnati, OH: St. Anthony Messenger Press, 1984.

Martin, Rafe, ed. *The Hungry Tigress: Buddhist Legends & Jataka Tales*. Berkeley, CA: Parallax Press, 1990.

McArdle, Jack. *150 Stories for Preachers and Teachers*. Mystic, CT: Twenty-Third Publications, 1990.

Mellon, Nancy. *Storytelling & the Art of Imagination*. Rockport, NY: Element, Inc., 1992.

Miller, Donald. *The Gospel and Mother Goose*. Elgin, IL: Brethren Press, 1987.

Minghella, Anthony, ed. *Jim Henson's The Storyteller*. NY: Borzoi–Alfred A. Knopf, Inc., 1991.

Newcombe, Jack. *A Christmas Treasury*. NY: Viking Press, 1982.

Night the Stars Sang, The: The Wonder That Is Christmas. Tarrytown, NY: Gleneida Publishing Group-Triumph Books, 1991 (by special arrangement with Guidepost Books).

Nomura, Yushi. *Desert Wisdom: Sayings from the Desert Fathers*. New York: Image Books, 1984.

O'Connor, Ulick. *Irish Tales & Sagas*. London: Dragon Books, 1985.

O'Faolain, Eileen. *Irish Sagas and Folk Tales*. NY: Avenel Books, 1982.

Olszewski, Daryl. *Balloons! Candy! Toys! and Other Parables for Storytellers*. San Jose, CA: Resource Publications, 1986.

Parry-Jones, D., ed. *Welsh Legends & Fairy Lore*. NY: Barnes & Noble–Marboro Books by arrangement with B.T. Batsford, Ltd., 1992.

Paulus, Trina. *Hope for the Flowers*. NJ: Paulist Press, 1972.

Pellowski, Anne. *The World of Storytelling*. Revised edition. NY: H.W. Wilson, 1990.

Pennel, Jr., Joe E. *The Whisper of Christmas: Reflections for Advent and Christmas*. Nashville: The Upper Room, 1984.

Powers, C.P., Isaias. *Nameless Faces in the Life of Jesus*. Mystic, CT: Twenty-Third Publications, 1981.

————. *Father Ike's Stories for Children*. Mystic, CT: Twenty-Third Publications, 1988.

Ramanujan, A.K., ed. *Folktales from India*. NY: Pantheon Books–Random House, 1991.

Reynolds, David K., Ph.D. *Playing Ball on Running Water*. NY: Quill, 1984.

————. *Even in Summers the Ice Doesn't Melt*. NY: Quill, 1986.

————. *Water Bears No Scars*. NY: Quill, 1987.

————. *Pools of Lodging for the Moon: Strategy for a Positive Life-Style*. NY: William Morrow & Co., 1989.

————. *A Thousand Waves: A Sensible Life-Style for Sensitive People*. NY: William Morrow & Co., 1990.

Seuss, Dr. *Oh, the Places You'll Go!* NY: Random House, 1990.

Shea, John. *The Spirit Master*. Chicago: Thomas More Press, 1987.

————. *Starlight: Beholding the Christmas Miracle All Year Long*. NY: Crossroad Publishing, 1992.

Singer, Isaac Bashevis. *Stories for Children*. NY: Farrar, Straus, Giroux, 1984.

————. *The Image and Other Stories*. London: Jonathan Cape, Ltd., 1985.

Smith, Richard Gordon. *Ancient Tales and Folklore of Japan*. London: Bracken Books, 1986.

Stoddard, Sandol. *The Rules and Mysteries of Brother Solomon*. Mahwah, NJ: Paulist Press, 1987.

Stromberg, Bob. *Why Geese Fly Farther Than Eagles.* Colorado Springs: Focus on the Family Publ., 1992.

Sutherland, Zena and Liningston, Myra Cohn, eds. *The Scott, Foresman Anthology of Children's Literature.* IL: Scott, Foresman and Co., 1984.

Tan, Paul Lee. *Encyclopedia of 7700 Illustrations: Signs of the Times.* Rockville, MD: Assurance Publishers, 1979.

Tazewell, Charles. *The Littlest Angel.* Nashville: Ideals Publishing, 1946.

Thoma, Clemens and Wyschogrod, Michael, ed. *Parable and Story in Judaism and Christianity.* Mahwah: Paulist Press, 1989.

Thompson, Stith. *The Folktale.* Los Angeles: The University of California Press, 1977.

Vecsey, Christopher. *Imagine Ourselves Richly: Mythic Narratives of North American Indians.* San Francisco: Harper–Collins, 1991.

Weinreich, Beatrice Silverman, ed. *Yiddish Folktales.* Translated by Leonard Wolf. NY: Pantheon-Random House, 1988.

Wharton, Paul, ed. *Stories and Parables for Preachers and Teachers.* NY: Paulist Press, 1986.

White, William R., ed. *Speaking in Stories.* Minneapolis: Augsburg, 1982.

————. *Stories for Telling.* Minneapolis: Augsburg, 1986.

————. *Stories for the Journey.* Minneapolis: Augsburg, 1988.

Wiesel, Elie. *Souls on Fire: Portraits and Legends of Hasidic Masters.* NY: Summit Books, 1972.

————. *Somewhere a Master: Further Hasidic Portraits and Legends.* NY: Summit Books, 1981.

Wilde, Oscar. *The Happy Prince and Other Fairy Tales.* NY: Dover, 1992.

Wood, Douglas. *Old Turtle.* Duluth, MN: Pfeifer–Hamilton Publishers, 1992.

Yolen, Jane, ed. *Favorite Folktales from Around the World.* NY: Pantheon Books–Random House, 1986.

Zipes, Jack, ed. *Spells of Enchantment: The Wondrous Fairy Tales of Western Culture.* NY: Viking–Penguin, 1991.
———. *Aesop's Fables . . . and 200 other famous fables.* NY: Signet Classic–Penguin, 1992.

Theme Index

110